CW01474866

**per
nary**

Primary Quizzes

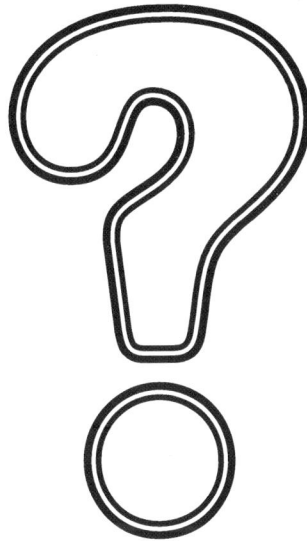

?

Written by Terry Johnson

Prim-Ed
Publishing

0755C

Published by R.I.C. Publications 2004
Reprinted under license in 2004 by Prim-Ed Publishing

Copyright© Terry Johnson 2004

ISBN 1 920962 15 8
PR–0755

Additional titles available in this series:
Primary Quizzes *(Lower Primary)*
Primary Quizzes *(Middle Primary)*

Internet websites
In some cases, websites or specific URLs may be recommended. While these are checked and rechecked at the time of publication, the publisher has no control over any subsequent changes which may be made to webpages. It is strongly recommended that the class teacher checks all URLs before allowing students to access them.

View all pages online

Email address: sales@prim-ed.com   Home page: www.prim-ed.com

Foreword

Primary Quizzes contains 40 educational quizzes aimed at expanding pupils' knowledge about their world. The questions cover a range of topics, including mathematics, language, history, technology and sport. General knowledge questions are also part of each quiz.

The quizzes can be presented and marked in a variety of ways, allowing pupils to work individually or in groups. Recording sheets are provided to record pupils' results. Suggestions for expanding the topics in each quiz are also provided, covering a range of curriculum and skill areas.

⋆✦ Contents

Teacher information

Construction of quizzes

Each of the 40 quizzes in this book contains 20 questions that are based on the following topics:

1.	Maths – number	11.	Famous people
2.	Animals	12.	General knowledge
3.	General knowledge	13.	Language – word study
4.	Historical events and places	14.	People of the world
5.	Language – grammar and spelling	15.	Performing arts
6.	General knowledge	16.	The environment
7.	Sport	17.	Literature
8.	Maths – space, measurement	18.	General knowledge
9.	Technology	19.	Our body
10.	Plants	20.	Geography

Each quiz is made up of a variety of question types. Some of the questions for each quiz use prompting to help pupils find the correct answer. Examples of the question types using prompting are:

- multiple choice
- missing words (e.g. 'A meat-eating plant is the Venus ...')
- true or false
- first letter provided (e.g. 'What, starting with 'w', is a unit of electrical power?')

The difficulty of the questions varies within each quiz, with some questions more likely to require access to resource materials (e.g. an atlas). Each question requires between a one- and three-word answer, with the majority requiring only one word. For most questions, there will only be one correct answer; however, the teacher may need to use his/her discretion in some cases.

Suggestions for presenting and expanding the quizzes

- Most quizzes may be given orally to the pupils by the teacher, but as some questions will require research or are visual, it is suggested the quizzes are photocopied to be answered by individual pupils or groups of pupils.

- Teachers may like to set up a weekly competition among groups of pupils.

- The quizzes may be made self-competitive, with each pupil plotting his/her progress from week to week (see page iv). A class record page, for teachers to record each pupil's results, is also provided (see page v).

- Teachers may mark each pupil's quiz or call out the correct answers for pupils to mark the quizzes themselves. This may also encourage debate about the answers.

- Teachers could give a time limit for the pupils to complete each quiz.

- Pupils may like to create their own quizzes to challenge the class with once they understand the format of the quizzes in this book.

- The 'Further Exploration' and 'Internet Challenges' given for each quiz could be expanded further by teachers or pupils. For example, teachers may wish pupils to complete an entire project on one of the topics.

Teacher information

A teachers page is provided for each quiz.

BEFORE THE QUIZ explains any difficult vocabulary contained in the questions that teachers may need to explain before pupils complete the quiz. A list of suggested resources pupils may need access to for each quiz is also provided. Note: It is assumed that dictionaries and encyclopedias will be available in the classroom when pupils are completing any of the quizzes.

ANSWERS for each quiz are provided. The answers to all of the quizzes are also found at the back of the book.

FURTHER EXPLORATION contains activity suggestions from a range of curriculum areas based on five of the questions from each quiz. Teachers may wish to use these with the whole class or allow individual pupils or small groups of pupils to complete one or more of the activities.

PRIMARY QUIZ 3 – TEACHERS NOTES

BEFORE THE QUIZ

Vocabulary
- Ensure pupils understand what 'common factors' and 'even numbers' are.
- Teachers may like to pronounce the word 'gendarme' for the pupils.
- Define the word 'gestation'.

Suggested resources
- Internet

ANSWERS

1.	3	11.	Ripper
2.	yes	12.	Roll
3.	police officer	13.	school
4.	Mandela	14.	(a)
5.	exercise	15.	music
6.	no	16.	fog
7.	game fishing	17.	Grimm
8.	72 m²	18.	tricycle
9.	true	19.	40
10.	Australia	20.	false

FURTHER EXPLORATION

Question 3	Write a list of French words that have become part of English.
Question 4	Deliver a speech about Nelson Mandela or another human rights activist.
Question 9	Discuss how a CD works. Ask pupils to imagine what technology might supersede it.
Question 13	Find some unusual collective nouns (e.g. 'a murder of crows') and create a quiz for the class.
Question 19	Research to find out the gestation periods of other animals. Rank them in order from shortest to longest.

6   Primary Quizzes   www.prim-ed.com   Prim-Ed Publishing

Each quiz contains 20 questions in a range of topic areas. Some questions provide prompting; e.g. multiple choice or true/false. Teachers should encourage pupils to write each answer on the line provided under each question for ease of marking.

DID YOU KNOW?, a snippet of additional information based on one of the questions, is provided for the pupils' interest. Teachers may like pupils to research other questions and provide their own snippets of information.

Suggestions for exploring the question selected for 'Did You Know' are provided in the form of an **INTERNET CHALLENGE**. The pupils can complete this individually or in small groups. Adult supervision will be required as pupils will need to use search engines.

Primary quiz 3

1. What is the common factor of both 24 and 27?

2. Are mammals warm-blooded?

3. Is a 'gendarme' a French shopkeeper, doctor or police officer?

4. Nelson ... was released from jail in South Africa in 1990.

5. Spell 'exercize' correctly.

6. Is half of 242 an even number?

7. In which recreation do competitors often use 'tag and release'?

8. What is the area of a rectangle nine metres long and eight metres wide?

9. The first compact disc (CD) was invented by Sony-Philips. True or false?

10. In which country will you find a blackbutt tree?

11. Murder was the reason why Jack the ... has became a household name throughout the world.

12. Complete this song title – *Shake, Rattle and ...*

13. Is a collection of fish called a school, a host or a fleet?

14. A state of everlasting peace called nirvana is a belief of:
    (a) Buddhists (b) Hindus (c) Muslims

15. In which arts form are you likely to see a 'diva'?

16. In the air it is called cloud, but on the ground it is called f...

17. *Cinderella* is one of the fairytales collected by the ... Brothers.

18. Is a 'becak' a type of unicycle, tandem cycle or tricycle?

19. If measured in weeks, how long is the normal human gestation period?

20. Thailand was originally called Persia. True or false?

/20

★ DID YOU KNOW?
The earliest version of the *Cinderella* story was found in a Chinese book written about 850 AD. The version we know was introduced in Europe in 1697.

INTERNET CHALLENGES
- Read about the origins of some other fairytales.
- Find out how many films have been made based on the *Cinderella* story.
- Find an early text and a modern text of *Cinderella* and compare them.

Prim-Ed Publishing   www.prim-ed.com   *Primary Quizzes*   7

✦★ My review page

Name _____

Quiz	Score/20	My Performance Rating			Comments
1		☺	😐	☹	
2		☺	😐	☹	
3		☺	😐	☹	
4		☺	😐	☹	
5		☺	😐	☹	
6		☺	😐	☹	
7		☺	😐	☹	
8		☺	😐	☹	
9		☺	😐	☹	
10		☺	😐	☹	
11		☺	😐	☹	
12		☺	😐	☹	
13		☺	😐	☹	
14		☺	😐	☹	
15		☺	😐	☹	
16		☺	😐	☹	
17		☺	😐	☹	
18		☺	😐	☹	
19		☺	😐	☹	
20		☺	😐	☹	
21		☺	😐	☹	
22		☺	😐	☹	
23		☺	😐	☹	
24		☺	😐	☹	
25		☺	😐	☹	
26		☺	😐	☹	
27		☺	😐	☹	
28		☺	😐	☹	
29		☺	😐	☹	
30		☺	😐	☹	
31		☺	😐	☹	
32		☺	😐	☹	
33		☺	😐	☹	
34		☺	😐	☹	
35		☺	😐	☹	
36		☺	😐	☹	
37		☺	😐	☹	
38		☺	😐	☹	
39		☺	😐	☹	
40		☺	😐	☹	

Primary Quizzes   www.prim-ed.com   Prim-Ed Publishing

★ Class record

Pupil's Name	1	2	3	4	5	6	7	8	9	10	11	12	13	14	15	16	17	18	19	20	21	22	23	24	25	26	27	28	29	30	31	32	33	34	35	36	37	38	39	40

PRIMARY QUIZ 1 – TEACHERS NOTES

BEFORE THE QUIZ

Vocabulary
*   Define a 'verb' and a 'syllable'.

Suggested resources
*   atlas, Internet

ANSWERS

1. 69
2. arachnid
3. alphabet
4. Boston
5. (c)
6. Blue
7. football
8. 12
9. heavier-than-air aircraft
10. yes

11. (a)
12. false
13. 3
14. Jewish
15. tempo
16. yes
17. Peter Benchley
18. incubator
19. ear
20. Austria

FURTHER EXPLORATION

Question 2   Research scorpions to find out how they capture their prey.

Question 3   Learn some letters of the Greek alphabet and find English words that have been derived from them.

Question 9   Write a biography of the Wright brothers.

Question 12   Write a list of facts about the blue whale.

Question 14   Draw a range of religious symbols and write the meaning of each.

Primary quiz 1

1. What is triple 23?

2. Is the scorpion an insect, an arachnid or neither of these?

3. Which word comes from combining the first two letters of the Greek alphabet?

4. In 1773, a group of locals dumped a cargo of tea from British ships that were anchored in which US harbour?

5. Which is not a verb?
   (a) catch   (b) manage   (c) active

6. Which sea does not exist – Black, Yellow, Blue, or Red?

7. In which game is Pelé regarded as possibly the greatest player ever?

8. How many edges does a cube have?

9. Orville and Wilbur Wright invented the first powered ...?

10. Does a deciduous tree drop its leaves?

11. Roald Amundsen and his team of explorers were the first to reach:
    (a) The South Pole
    (b) The North Pole
    (c) The peak of Mt Everest

12. To swim, whales move their tails from side to side. True or false?

13. How many syllables does the word 'submarine' have?

14. The Star of David is a symbol relevant to which people?

15. What term, starting with t, is used to describe how fast or slow a song is?

16. Does using fossil fuels like coal lead to an increase in acid rain?

17. Who wrote *Jaws* – Peter Benchley, Steven Spielberg or George Lucas?

18. A chicken is hatched in an *i*...

19. Where are the body's smallest bones located?

20. Which is a European country – Algeria, Austria or Argentina?

/20

★ **DID YOU KNOW?**

When we are born, our skeleton is made up of about 275 bones. As we grow, some of our bones fuse together. This leaves an adult with only 206 bones!

INTERNET CHALLENGES

O Find a model of the human skeleton.
O Find out which is the largest bone in the human body.
O Write the names of at least six bones in the adult human body.
O Find some examples of bones that fuse together during childhood.

PRIMARY QUIZ 2 – TEACHERS NOTES

BEFORE THE QUIZ

Vocabulary

• Teachers may like to pronounce the word 'eucalyptus' for pupils.

Suggested resources

• atlas, Internet, chart of the human body

ANSWERS

1. 84
2. mosquito
3. tree
4. 20th
5. yes
6. aorta
7. Tour de France
8. 36
9. sound/sight
10. Christmas
11. Russia
12. true
13. weighed
14. South America
15. red/yellow/blue
16. Yellow
17. lean
18. Submarine
19. orchid
20. Sea

FURTHER EXPLORATION

Question 7   Write a biography of a cyclist in the Tour de France.

Question 10 Write a report on the different Christmas customs followed around the world.

Question 15 Create a painting using only primary colours. The primary colours can be mixed together to create new colours.

Question 18 Play Beatles songs and give your opinion of one of them.

Question 19 Complete a diagram of the eye and explain how we see images.

Primary quiz 2

1. How many days are there in 12 weeks?

   _____

2. Which insect spreads malaria?

   _____

3. What is a 'eucalyptus gum?'

   _____

4. The Berlin Wall was torn down in which century – 19th, 20th, or 21st?

   _____

5. Is the apostrophe in this sentence in the correct place? *The man's uniform*.

   _____

6. What is the main artery in our body?

   _____

7. In which sporting event does the leader wear a yellow jersey?

   _____

8. How many years are there between 2004 and 1968?

   _____

9. 'Audiovisual' is made up of two words meaning *s*... and *s*... .

   _____

10. A decorated Norway spruce signifies what time of the year?

    _____

11. Catherine the Great was a German princess who ended up ruling *R*... .

    _____

12. Arabic is written from right to left. True or false?

    _____

13. Which is third in alphabetical order – weight, wait, way, weighed?

    _____

14. In which continent might you see guinea pig on the menu?

    _____

15. What are the three primary colours?

    _____

16. The world's first national park was declared in the USA in 1872. It was named *...stone* National Park.

    _____

17. Jack Sprat's wife could eat no ... .

    _____

18. Complete this Beatles song title – *Yellow ...* .

    _____

19. Pick the odd one out – retina, pupil, orchid, iris.

    _____

20. The Tasman ... lies between Australia and New Zealand.

    _____

    /20

★ **DID YOU KNOW?**

The Berlin Wall was a 162-kilometre (approx.) wall that separated East Berlin (part of East Germany) from West Berlin (part of West Germany).

INTERNET CHALLENGES

O Find a picture of the remains of the Berlin Wall. How much is left?

O Find out why the Berlin Wall was built and how it eventually fell.

O Read a story of a family which was separated by the Berlin Wall.

O View some pictures of the day the Wall came down.

O Find out about some other tourist attractions in Berlin.

PRIMARY QUIZ 3 – TEACHERS NOTES

BEFORE THE QUIZ

Vocabulary
*   Ensure pupils understand what 'common factors' and 'even numbers' are.
*   Teachers may like to pronounce the word 'gendarme' for the pupils.
*   Define the word 'gestation'.

Suggested resources
*   Internet

ANSWERS

1. 3
2. yes
3. police officer
4. Mandela
5. exercise
6. no
7. game fishing
8. 72 m^2
9. true
10. Australia
11. Ripper
12. Roll
13. school
14. (a)
15. music
16. fog
17. Grimm
18. tricycle
19. 40
20. false

FURTHER EXPLORATION

Question 3	Write a list of French words that have become part of English.
Question 4	Deliver a speech about Nelson Mandela or another human rights activist.
Question 9	Discuss how a CD works. Ask pupils to imagine what technology might supersede it.
Question 13	Find some unusual collective nouns (e.g. 'a murder of crows') and create a quiz for the class.
Question 19	Research to find out the gestation periods of other animals. Rank them in order from shortest to longest.

Primary quiz 3

1. What is the common factor of both 24 and 27?

2. Are mammals warm-blooded?

3. Is a 'gendarme' a French shopkeeper, doctor or police officer?

4. Nelson ... was released from jail in South Africa in 1990.

5. Spell 'exercize' correctly.

6. Is half of 242 an even number?

7. In which recreation do competitors often use 'tag and release'?

8. What is the area of a rectangle nine metres long and eight metres wide?

9. The first compact disc (CD) was invented by Sony-Philips. True or false?

10. In which country will you find a blackbutt tree?

11. Murder was the reason why Jack the ... has became a household name throughout the world.

12. Complete this song title – *Shake, Rattle and ...*

13. Is a collection of fish called a school, a host or a fleet?

14. A state of everlasting peace called nirvana is a belief of:
(a) Buddhists   (b) Hindus   (c) Muslims

15. In which arts form are you likely to see a 'diva?'

16. In the air it is called cloud, but on the ground it is called *f*...

17. *Cinderella* is one of the fairytales collected by the ... Brothers.

18. Is a 'becak' a type of unicycle, tandem cycle or tricycle?

19. If measured in weeks, how long is the normal human gestation period?

20. Thailand was originally called Persia. True or false?

/20

★ **DID YOU KNOW?**
The earliest version of the *Cinderella* story was found in a Chinese book written about 850 AD. The version we know was introduced in Europe in 1697.

INTERNET CHALLENGES
O Read about the origins of some other fairytales.
O Find out how many films have been made based on the *Cinderella* story.
O Find an early text and a modern text of *Cinderella* and compare them.

PRIMARY QUIZ 4 – TEACHERS NOTES

BEFORE THE QUIZ

Vocabulary
- Ensure pupils understand what an adjective is.
- Ensure pupils understand what 'prime numbers' and 'squared numbers' are.
- Define the term 'biome'.

Suggested resources
- Internet, chart of the human skeleton

ANSWERS

1. 121
2. ostrich
3. General Custer
4. false
5. spare
6. singer
7. Jonny Wilkinson
8. 1.8 L
9. television
10. mushroom/fungus
11. George Washington
12. 53
13. d
14. New Zealand
15. (b)
16. (a)
17. 7
18. nerves
19. shoulder
20. Scandinavia

FURTHER EXPLORATION

Question 4	Invite a visually-impaired guest speaker to explain how he/she reads braille. The pupils could also try to read simple words in braille.
Question 6/7	Write a fact file about Buddy Holly or Jonny Wilkinson.
Question 17	Write lyrics for a comedy version of *The 12 Days of Christmas*.
Question 19	Label a chart of the human skeleton with the major bones of the body.
Question 20	Design a four-week tour of Scandinavia, visiting all the major tourist attractions.

Primary quiz 4

1. What is 11 squared?

2. Which bird lays the largest eggs?

3. Which general died at Little Big Horn?

4. The Louis Braille system to help blind people read was invented in 1929. True or false?

5. Which is the adjective in this sentence? 'She sat down hurriedly at the spare desk.'

6. Was Buddy Holly a famous writer, actor or singer?

7. Which England rugby player secured victory with his drop-kick, in the final of 2003 Rugby World Cup?

8. If a fish tank held 6.5 L before and 4.7 L after, how much water has been displaced?

9. John Logie Baird is credited as being the 'father' of ...?

10. 'Death Cap' is the name given to the world's deadliest what?

11. Who was the first president of the United States?

12. What is the first prime number after 50?

13. Which letter is silent in handkerchief?

14. The Maori people are native to which country?

15. The theme for *The Simpsons* was written by
    (a) Francis Scott Key
    (b) Danny Elfman
    (c) Jerry Goldsmith

16. The richest of all biomes are:
    (a) the tropical rainforests
    (b) temperate rainforests
    (c) the grasslands.

17. How many 'swans-a-swimming' did my true love send to me?

18. Is neurology the study of bones, muscles or nerves?

19. Would you find the scapula in the knee, shoulder or wrist?

20. Where would you see the spectacular 'Land of the Midnight Sun' – the Caribbean, the Himalayas or Scandinavia?

/20

★ **DID YOU KNOW?**

Traditional Maori people of high classes wore *moko* (tattoos). These were made using bone chisels and mallets. Women had them on their chins and lips and men covered their faces and other parts of their bodies with them.

INTERNET CHALLENGES

O Find some pictures of traditional Maori designs.
O Write a list of Maori words and their meanings.
O Read some Maori legends.

PRIMARY QUIZ 5 – TEACHERS NOTES

BEFORE THE QUIZ

Vocabulary

- Define the words 'shrine' and 'acronym'.
- Teachers may like to pronounce the words 'Borobudur', 'Bonaparte', 'Tahitians', 'Polynesia', 'Elephantiasis' and 'Buenos Aires' for pupils.

Suggested resources

- Internet, atlas

ANSWERS

1. one third
2. troops
3. Arthur
4. Indonesia
5. y
6. Spain
7. chalk
8. none
9. gigabyte
10. true
11. Napoleon
12. whip
13. (b)
14. true
15. Bilbo Baggins
16. World Health Organization
17. Horse
18. no
19. true
20. Argentina

FURTHER EXPLORATION

Question 3 Read stories about King Arthur and try writing your own.

Question 6 Imagine you visit Pamplona. Write a narrative describing your participation in or observation of the Running of the Bulls.

Question 7 Design an outdoor game based on the scoring system of billiards or snooker.

Question 14 Create a travel brochure for Tahiti.

Question 15 Write a description of a mythical world that could be used as the setting of a fantasy novel.

Primary quiz 5

1. What fraction is the equivalent of 33%?

2. Do monkeys live in groups called mobs, packs or troops?

3. Which king had a magic sword named Excalibur?

4. Borobudur is one of the world's greatest Buddhist shrines, located in which country?

5. In the word 'oxygen', which letter makes the 'ee' sound?

6. In which country can you 'run with the bulls'?

7. What substance is put on the end of the cue when playing billiards?

8. How many equal sides does a scalene triangle have?

9. Which is bigger – a megabyte or a gigabyte?

10. Cork is the bark of the cork oak. True or false?

11. One of the most outstanding soldiers in modern history was ... Bonaparte.

12. What is a 'cat of nine tails'?

13. Which word uses the prefix 'ir'?
    (a) reckless   (b) regular   (c) real

14. The Tahitians live in a region called Polynesia. True or false?

15. What is Frodo's cousin's name?

16. WHO is an acronym for what?

17. An Arabian Nights story title is 'The Story of the Enchanted ...'.

18. Would a hungry tiger be docile?

19. The syndrome called 'Elephantiasis', in which the arms and legs can grow to elephantoid size, is caused by a roundworm. True or false?

20. Buenos Aires is the capital city of ...

/20

★ **DID YOU KNOW?**

It is thought that only about 5000 to 7000 tigers are left in the wild, making the tiger an endangered species. Balinese, Javan and Caspian tigers are already extinct.

INTERNET CHALLENGES

O Find out which subspecies of tigers are still alive today.

O Find pictures of different types of tigers.

O Write a list of facts about one type of tiger.

O Find out reasons why some subspecies of tigers have become extinct.

PRIMARY QUIZ 6 – TEACHERS NOTES

BEFORE THE QUIZ

Vocabulary

• Ensure pupils understand what 'square numbers', 'pronouns' and 'synonyms' are.

• Teachers may like to pronounce the words 'Krakatoa', 'Montgolfier', 'Cerebral haemorrhage' and 'Hiroshima' for pupils.

Suggested resources

• thesaurus, Internet, atlas

ANSWERS

1. no
2. giraffe
3. doctor
4. Indonesia
5. off
6. 144
7. high jump
8. yes
9. hot air balloon
10. grass/weed/lawn
11. Dickens
12. Australia
13. (c)
14. Russia
15. false
16. better
17. the tarts
18. country
19. brain
20. Japan

FURTHER EXPLORATION

Question 3 Create a healthy diet and exercise plan for someone your age.

Question 9 Research to find out how hot air balloons work.

Question 11 Watch the film *Oliver Twist* and write a review.

Question 14 Listen to the traditional music used for dances from a range of cultures. Create a movement piece to one of them in a small group.

Question 20 Read a history of the city of Hiroshima.

Primary quiz 6

1. Is 500 a square number?

2. Which is taller – an elephant or a giraffe?

3. To solve an obesity problem, would you consult a mechanic, a lawyer or a doctor?

4. The world's loudest volcanic explosion occurred in 1883 in which country, when the island of Krakatoa blew itself apart?

5. Which is not a pronoun – he, they, off, you?

6. How many eggs are there in 12 dozen?

7. In which sporting event did Dick Fosbury create the 'Fosbury Flop?'

8. Will a carpet measuring 5 metres x 5 metres fit into a living room of 30 square metres?

9. Did the Montgolfier Brothers fly the first hot air balloon or first airship?

10. What is 'couch'?

11. One of England's greatest novelists was Charles D...

12. In which country is a product called Vegemite™ spread onto bread?

13. Which word is a synonym for 'quaint'?
    (a) real   (b) queer   (c) odd

14. Cossack dancing is a part of which country's culture?

15. A pantomime is the musical composition for an orchestra. True or false?

16. If more people used public transport, would it be better for the environment or worse?

17. What did the Knave of Hearts steal?

18. Someone who commits treason betrays his/her …

19. Where in the body would a 'cerebral haemorrhage' occur?

20. Hiroshima is a city in which country?

/20

★ **DID YOU KNOW?**
Volcanic eruptions can trigger tsunamis, earthquakes, floods, rockfalls and mudflows!

INTERNET CHALLENGES
O Find aerial photographs of volcanoes.
O Find out the names of some active volcanoes in the world.
O When did the last volcano in the world erupt and what damage did it cause?

PRIMARY QUIZ 7 – TEACHERS NOTES

BEFORE THE QUIZ

Vocabulary

- Ensure pupils understand what 'square numbers' and 'palindromes' are.
- Teachers may like to pronounce the words 'Irian Jaya', 'Kombai' and 'Korowai' for pupils.

Suggested resources

- atlas, Internet

ANSWERS

1. 6.84
2. nocturnal
3. yes
4. Gettysburg
5. king
6. no
7. 45
8. 10 000
9. Karl Benz
10. cedar
11. Hans Christian Andersen
12. race(horse)
13. gather (hard 'g')
14. (c)
15. Chaplin
16. acidic
17. *Little Women*
18. long
19. eyes
20. false

FURTHER EXPLORATION

Question 2 If possible, visit a zoo and write observations about the features of nocturnal animals.

Question 6 Investigate palindromes involving sentences or phrases (e.g. 'Was it a rat I saw?'). Make a list of palindromic words and ask pupils to try devising their own palindromic sentences.

Question 11 Write a biography of the life of Hans Christian Andersen.

Question 15 Watch footage of Charlie Chaplin and other physical comedians such as Rowan Atkinson. Create physical comedies in small groups.

Question 16 Locate countries prone to acid rain on a map of the world.

Primary quiz 7

1. Which is the largest number – 6.48, 6.84, 6.8, 6.6?

2. What do we call animals that only come out at night?

3. Is 400 a square number?

4. On 1–3 July 1863, the greatest battle of the American Civil War took place at …

5. Which word does not need a capital? King, April, California, Renae

6. Is the word 'river' an example of a palindrome?

7. How many minutes are there in each half of an international football game?

8. How many square metres are there in one hectare?

9. Who sold the first ever car – Karl Benz or Henry Ford?

10. Unjumble CREAD to make the name of a type of tree.

11. The statue of the 'Little Mermaid' in Copenhagen, Denmark, is dedicated to which Danish author of fairytales?

12. What is, or was, Sea Biscuit?

13. Which is the odd one out – giant, gentle, gather, germs?

14. The houses of Irian Jaya's Kombai and Korowai tribes can be built at an amazingly high:
    (a) 15 metres above the ground
    (b) 30 metres above the ground
    (c) 45 metres above the ground

15. A superstar of early films was a little Englishman called Charlie …

16. Is acid rain far more radioactive, acidic or gaseous than normal rain?

17. Jo, Amy, Beth and Meg are all characters from which Louisa May Alcott novel?

18. An LP record, popular before CDs, is a … playing record.

19. An optician is a specialist in which body part?

20. The Equator passes through Norway. True or false?

/20

★ **DID YOU KNOW?**

As well as the Little Mermaid statue, Denmark is also home to LEGOLAND©. This is an amusement park that has been built from 40 million pieces of LEGO©!

INTERNET CHALLENGES

O Find a city map of Copenhagen and locate its major tourist attractions.
O Write the names of other famous Danish people and their achievements.
O Write some common Danish words and their meanings.
O Find some recipes for traditional Danish food.

PRIMARY QUIZ 8 – TEACHERS NOTES

BEFORE THE QUIZ

Vocabulary

- Ensure pupils understand what the word 'tessellate' means.
- Teachers may like to pronounce the words 'Koi' and 'archipelago' for pupils.

Suggested resources

- atlas, hexagonal shapes, Internet

ANSWERS

1. 43
2. true
3. 1 mile
4. Stonehenge
5. were
6. throw
7. tennis
8. yes
9. General Electric Company
10. yes
11. Van Gogh
12. 50s
13. churches
14. Japan
15. painting
16. positive
17. bread
18. piccolo
19. sugar
20. true

FURTHER EXPLORATION

Question 4 Read various theories on the origins of Stonehenge and then write your own.

Question 8 Create a tessellating tile design for a bathroom.

Question 11 View Van Gogh paintings on the Internet. Choose the one you like the best and explain why.

Question 18 Invite musicians from an orchestra to play different instruments for the pupils.

Question 20 Write a list of facts about the culture of Indonesia.

Primary quiz 8

1. What is one-third of 129?

   _____

2. Hyenas are scavengers. True or false?

   _____

3. Which is further – one kilometre or one mile?

   _____

4. An ancient and mystical stone structure located in the south of England is called ...

   _____

5. Which word is wrong in this sentence? 'A packet of crisps were found on the bench'.

   _____

6. Would you eat, wear or throw a 'boomerang?'

   _____

7. Bjorn Borg was a champion ... player from Sweden.

   _____

8. Will a hexagonal tile tessellate?

   _____

9. Which company, known as GEC, invented the electric toaster?

   _____

10. We know bees transfer pollen, but can bats do the same?

    _____

11. Which great Dutch painter, with the first name of Vincent, cut off one of his ear lobes?

    _____

12. In which decade did the bikini first become popular – 50s, 60s or 70s?

    _____

13. Write the plural of church.

    _____

14. The Koi fish is known as the 'traditional fish of happiness' and therefore would most likely be found at a wedding reception in which country?

    _____

15. 'Abstract' is a term generally associated with which arts form?

    _____

16. Would 'sustainable development' be a positive or negative for the environment?

    _____

17. The Old Woman in a Shoe gave her children some broth without any ...

    _____

18. What is the smallest instrument in an orchestra?

    _____

19. Diabetes affects the body's ability to use what?

    _____

20. Indonesia is the world's largest archipelago. True or false?

    _____

                                                    /20

★ **DID YOU KNOW?**

The spotted hyena has such powerful jaws it can crush large bones with its teeth. It also makes a loud 'cackling' sound, from where it gets its more common name – the 'laughing' hyena.

INTERNET CHALLENGES

O Find out the names of other types of hyenas and locate where they live.

O Find out which animals hyenas are most closely related to.

O Listen to the sound a 'laughing' hyena makes.

O View pictures of hyenas.

PRIMARY QUIZ 9 – TEACHERS NOTES

BEFORE THE QUIZ

Vocabulary
- Define the words 'proper noun' and 'contraction'.
- Teachers may like to pronounce the words 'boules', 'chlorophyll' and 'tempera' for pupils.

Suggested resources
- Internet, atlas

ANSWERS

1. 4
2. greyhound
3. Snoopy
4. (a)
5. Kate
6. 11
7. France
8. 0105 hrs
9. no
10. chlorophyll
11. Sherlock Holmes
12. Edmund Hillary
13. beneath
14. people of the USSR
15. true
16. false
17. Mary Poppins
18. 420
19. blood
20. Tanzania

FURTHER EXPLORATION

Question 3	Create your own cartoon strip.
Question 6	Interview grandparents or other people who witnessed the first moon landing on television. Find out how they felt watching it.
Question 7	Play boules, petanque or bocce in teams.
Question 11	Write a biography of Arthur Conan Doyle.
Question 16	Write a report about some adaptations of desert plants and animals.

Primary quiz 9

1. Round 3.7 to the nearest whole number.

2. What is the fastest breed of dog?

3. What is the name of Charlie Brown's dog?

4. The Great Pyramids of Egypt were built in approximately:
   (a) 2700 BC – 2500 BC
   (b) 600 BC – 400 BC
   (c) 200 AD – 400 AD

5. Which is the proper noun in this sentence? 'Kate unwrapped her birthday present'.

6. The rocket which took Neil Armstrong to the moon was Apollo ...

7. 'Boules' originates from which country?

8. Change this time to 24-hour time – 1.05 am

9. In technological terms, is a 'malfunction' a good thing?

10. Do leaves get their colour from a green pigment called chlorine, chlorophyll or chloride?

11. Which fictitious detective lived at 221B Baker Street, London?

12. Who was Tenzing Norgay's partner?

13. What is the meaning of the contraction "'neath"?

14. Which people lived in fear of the KGB?

15. 'Tempera' is a painting term. True or false?

16. Deserts make up about 35% of the earth's landmass. True or false?

17. With which fictional character do you associate Cherry Tree Lane?

18. How many seconds in seven minutes?

19. A reading of '120 over 80' would apply to ... pressure.

20. Which is an African country – Thailand, Turkey or Tanzania?

/20

★ **DID YOU KNOW?**

The Pyramids were constructed as the burial places of pharaohs. They pointed upwards so a pharaoh could join the gods in the afterlife.

INTERNET CHALLENGES

O View pictures of some of the Pyramids.
O Find out some fascinating facts about the religious beliefs of the ancient Egyptians.
O Find the names of three Egyptian pharaohs and what they achieved.
O Discover some other tourist attractions in Egypt.

PRIMARY QUIZ 10 – TEACHERS NOTES

BEFORE THE QUIZ

Vocabulary
•   Ensure pupils understand the words 'superlative' and 'synonym'.

Suggested resources
•   thesaurus, Internet, book of flags

ANSWERS

1. 3600
2. lodge
3. eggs
4. 1969
5. happiness
6. African
7. wrestling
8. yes
9. ballpoint pen
10. (c)

11. Pasteur
12. scent
13. hottest
14. (a)
15. musical instrument
16. pressure
17. plum
18. plant
19. (b)
20. saffron (orange)

FURTHER EXPLORATION

Question 2   Create a flow chart to show how a beaver builds a lodge.

Question 9   Find out about the origins of 'everyday' inventions; e.g. paperclips, zips.

Question 14   Invite guest speakers to talk about festivals celebrated in their home countries.

Question 17   Research the origin of different nursery rhymes (e.g. Ring-a-ring-a-rosy is associated with the black death and Little Jack Horner has political connotations).

Question 20   Design a new flag for a country of your choice, after researching its history, people, natural resources, physical features and tourist attractions.

Primary quiz 10

1. How many seconds are there in one hour – 360, 600, 3600 or 6000?

2. A beaver's home is called a *l*...

3. What is the basic ingredient of an omelette?

4. In what year did a human walk on the moon for the first time?

5. Unjumble this word, ending in 'ness': **spanipehs**

6. Which is bigger – the African or Asian elephant?

7. In what sport does the loser get 'pinned'?

8. Do these rectangles have the same perimeter – 12 metres x 4 metres and 13 metres x 3 metres?

9. What did Laszlo and Georg Biro create?

10. Which is not a type of flowering plant?
    (a) protea   (b) begonia
    (c) sequoia   (d) fuchsia

11. To keep milk germ-free, Louis ... created pasteurised milk.

12. Which is a synonym of 'aroma' – scent, sent or cent?

13. What is the superlative form of hot?

14. A Japanese festival called 'O-Bon' is also known as the Festival for the
    (a) Dead   (b) Spirits   (c) Gods

15. What are castanets?

16. Winds are produced when there is a difference in what?

17. What did Little Jack Horner pull out with his thumb?

18. What is a rhododendron?

19. The bubonic plague is a disease caused by the infestation of which insect?
    (a) mosquito   (b) flea   (c) Tsetse fly

20. India's flag is coloured green, white and ...

/20

★ **DID YOU KNOW?**

In the 14th century, the bubonic plague, or 'black death', killed more than one-third of the entire population of Europe.

INTERNET CHALLENGES

O Find out what symptoms a person with bubonic plague will have.

O What did people do to try to prevent getting bubonic plague in the 14th century?

O Find out if bubonic plague is still a problem today.

PRIMARY QUIZ 11 – TEACHERS NOTES

BEFORE THE QUIZ

Vocabulary
- Define the words 'abbreviation', 'consonants', 'homophone' and 'singular'.
- Teachers may like to pronounce the word 'Tiananmen' for pupils.

Suggested resources
- atlas, chart of the human body, Internet

ANSWERS

1. 35
2. odour
3. Incorporated
4. China
5. 5
6. glacier
7. 20
8. 21 hours
9. Memory
10. bouquets
11. Nobel Prize / dynamite
12. knead
13. foot
14. Mexico
15. Star Trek
16. (c)
17. *Baggy*
18. 60s
19. skin
20. Mediterranean

FURTHER EXPLORATION

Question 3   Write a list of common abbreviations and hold a quiz on them.

Question 6   Locate the world's largest glaciers on a map of the world.

Question 11   Choose a past Nobel Prize winner. Write an acceptance speech as if you were that person.

Question 14   Prepare a party with a Mexican theme for a class of younger pupils.

Question 20   Imagine you have visited Cyprus. Write a diary entry for one of the days you were there.

Primary quiz 11

1. Take 64 from 99.

2. The skunk defends itself with a fluid that has a really bad *o*...

3. What does the abbreviation 'Inc.' stand for?

4. In 1989, protests in Tiananmen Square turned ugly when authorities in which country massacred over 1500 people?

5. How many consonants are there in the word 'python'?

6. What is a slow moving river of ice called?

7. Excluding the bullseyes, how many numbers are on a dartboard?

8. How many hours are there between 4 pm Monday and 1 pm Tuesday?

9. In computer jargon, RAM stands for Random Access ...

10. Flowers bunched together are called and pronounced 'boo-kays'. Spell this correctly.

11. What legacy did the Swedish inventor Alfred Nobel leave to the world?

12. Spell correctly the homophone of 'need'.

13. What is the singular form of 'feet?'

14. Flat corn pancakes called tortillas and folded ones called tacos are basic foods in which North American country?

15. On which TV show will you see a Vulcan named Spock?

16. Which is not a part of the water cycle?
(a) evaporation   (b) transpiration
(c) conservation   (d) condensation

17. K & B Jackson wrote the story, *The Saggy ... Elephant*.

18. The beginning of the hippie era is associated with which decade?

19. What is the largest organ of the body?

20. The island country of Cyprus is in which sea?

/20

★ **DID YOU KNOW?**

Believe it or not, some people in the USA keep skunks as pets! The skunks have had their musk glands removed so they cannot defend themselves by spraying.

INTERNET CHALLENGES

O Find a website that gives advice on keeping a skunk as a pet.

O Which animals are most closely related to the skunk?

O Find out what sort of diet a skunk in the wild has.

O Find out where skunks live.

PRIMARY QUIZ 12 – TEACHERS NOTES

BEFORE THE QUIZ

Vocabulary
*   Define the words 'cubed' and 'perimeter'.
*   Teachers may like to pronounce the word 'Salzburg' for pupils.

Suggested resources
*   Internet

ANSWERS

1. 27
2. bamboo
3. Athens
4. true
5. question mark
6. planets
7. yachting
8. 32 m
9. IBM-compatible
10. stamen
11. Elizabeth II
12. lion
13. (b)
14. (b)
15. false
16. true
17. Secret Garden
18. lilac
19. heights
20. true

FURTHER EXPLORATION

Question 3   Prepare an Olympic Games submission for a city you think should hold the next Games. Include details of its attractions.

Question 10 Research to find out the methods plants use to reproduce.

Question 11 Write a time line of events in Queen Elizabeth II's life.

Question 17 Role play scenes from *The Secret Garden*.

Question 20 Design new paper currency for your home country.

Primary quiz 12

1. What is 3 cubed?

_____

2. Which plant does the giant panda usually feed on?

_____

3. In which city were the 2004 Olympic Games held?

_____

4. The Great Wall of China was built before Christ was born. True or false?

_____

5. What is missing from this sentence? 'Are you going to the party' she asked.

_____

6. MVEMJSUNP are the first letters of the nine ...

_____

7. In which sport do countries compete for the America's Cup?

_____

8. What is the perimeter of a square with 8-m sides?

_____

9. Is 'Windows '98®' compatible with IBM-compatible or Apple computers?

_____

10. The male reproductive organ of a flower is called the *st*...

_____

11. Which Elizabeth succeeded George VI to the British throne?

_____

12. Which animal lives in groups called prides?

_____

13. What is a collection of flowers called?
(a) vase   (b) bouquet   (c) basket

_____

14. Deepavali (The Festival of the Lights) is a festival celebrated by:
(a) Buddhists (b) Hindus (c) Muslims

_____

15. Salsa dancing originates from Salzburg, Austria. True or false?

_____

16. Generally speaking, the older the ecosystem the more species it is likely to contain. True or false?

_____

17. Mary Lennox was the young girl who found the key to the what?

_____

18. Which is a pale purple colour – maroon, lilac or musk?

_____

19. Vertigo is a fear of what?

_____

20. The 'yen' is the currency of Japan. True or false?

_____

/20

★ **DID YOU KNOW?**
Deepavali or Diwali, is dedicated to the goddess Lakshmi. During Deepavali, some of the things people do include praying, offering sweets to Lakshmi at shrines and giving cards to their friends.

INTERNET CHALLENGES
O Find out what other traditions are followed during Deepavali.
O Find a picture of the goddess Lakshmi and other gods of the Hindu faith.
O Find out where Deepavali is celebrated.

PRIMARY QUIZ 13 – TEACHERS NOTES

BEFORE THE QUIZ

Vocabulary

*   Ensure pupils understand the terms 'prime numbers', 'nouns' and 'syllables'.
*   Teachers may like to pronounce the words 'Machu Picchu', 'capillaries', 'Zambezi' and 'Mekong' for pupils.

Suggested resources

*   atlas, Internet

ANSWERS

1. yes
2. ostrich
3. Spain
4. tube
5. pronoun
6. green
7. volleyball
8. 6 L
9. telephone
10. pumpkin
11. Nightingale
12. Peru
13. alphabetical
14. false
15. film/theatre
16. ozone layer
17. and all things nice
18. the clock
19. blood vessels
20. Caspian

FURTHER EXPLORATION

Question 6   Devise your own board game. Include a list of instructions.

Question 10 Bring a range of unusual fruits to the classroom. Ask pupils to taste test them and write their opinions.

Question 12 Write a list of interesting information about Machu Picchu, suitable for a website on South America.

Question 16 Design a poster that informs people about ozone layer depletion.

Question 20 Write a list of 'river records'; e.g. the longest river, the shortest river, the deepest river.

Primary quiz 13

1. Is 31 a prime number?

2. Which land animal has the largest eyes – ostrich, elephant or grizzly bear?

3. Which is the only country to border Portugal – Spain, France or Morocco?

4. In 1978, the world's first 'test … baby' was born.

5. A … is a word used in the place of a noun.

6. In the game of Monopoly®, what colour is the property of Bond St?

7. In which sport can you 'spike' the ball over the net?

8. What is the total capacity of four containers each holding 1.5 L of water?

9. What did Alexander Graham Bell invent?

10. What is generally regarded as being the world's largest fruit?

11. Probably the world's most famous nurse was Florence who?

12. Is Machu Picchu in Peru, Chile or Columbia?

13. Which word has more syllables – 'unbreakable' or 'alphabetical'?

14. Traditional polka dancing originated in Poland. True or false?

15. In which arts form would you hear the term 'a cameo performance'?

16. In 1985, a hole in the … was discovered over Antarctica.

17. What are little girls made of besides sugar and spice …?

18. What did Bill Haley rock around in 1955?

19. Are capillaries muscles, nerves or blood vessels?

20. Which is the odd one out – Volga, Zambezi, Mekong, Caspian?

/20

★ **DID YOU KNOW?**

Monopoly® was invented by American Charles B Darrow in 1934. It was rejected initially by Parker Brothers, the company that would one day produce it, due to 52 design errors!

INTERNET CHALLENGES
O Find out what the most popular board games in the world are.
O Find a website for people who love playing Monopoly®.
O Find out how Monopoly® has been modified from its original form.

PRIMARY QUIZ 14 – TEACHERS NOTES

BEFORE THE QUIZ

Vocabulary

- Define the word 'homophone'.
- Teachers may like to pronounce the words 'philatelist' and 'Schumacher' for pupils.

Suggested resources

- Internet, atlas, chart of the human skeleton

ANSWERS

1. 1000
2. land/water
3. *Titanic*
4. 16th
5. tomatoes
6. stamps
7. Formula 1/car racing
8. 3400
9. 8 (1961 – 1969)
10. true
11. Mark Spitz
12. eat/gulp/etc.
13. paw
14. Italy
15. *The Lion King*
16. balance
17. bear
18. nanny
19. femur
20. false

FURTHER EXPLORATION

Question 2	If possible, watch a frog develop from a tadpole in the classroom.
Question 6	Design a new stamp that commemorates the anniversary of your school opening.
Question 11	Write a list of amazing Olympic records.
Question 14	Make Italian food for a class party.
Question 19	Compile a fact file about bones.

Primary quiz 14

1. Write ten hundreds as a numeral.

   _____

2. Amphibians can live on both … and in …

   _____

3. Which film grossed more – *Titanic* or *The Lion King*?

   _____

4. Michelangelo sculpted his statue of David at the beginning of the 14th, 16th or 20th century?

   _____

5. Which is the correct spelling – tomatose, tomatos, tomatoes?

   _____

6. What does a philatelist collect?

   _____

7. Michael Schumacher is a name associated with which sport?

   _____

8. 3.4 kilograms = … grams

   _____

9. How many years between the first manned space flight and humans landing on the moon – 8, 14 or 22?

   _____

10. A hybrid is a cross between two species. True or false?

    _____

11. Which American became famous in 1972 when he won an amazing seven Olympic Gold medals in swimming?

    _____

12. To 'wolf it down' is a figure of speech meaning to … something quickly?

    _____

13. 'Pore' and 'pour' are homophones of 'poor'. Write another one.

    _____

14. I would be in … if the menu items were pasta, pizza, gelato and frutta?

    _____

15. Which film is the song 'Hakuna Matata' from?

    _____

16. In many countries, the introduction of feral species has caused a huge disruption in the *b*… of nature.

    _____

17. What kind of animal is Paddington?

    _____

18. What word can describe both a person who looks after young children and a grandmother?

    _____

19. What is the longest bone in the body?

    _____

20. Canada borders Mexico. True or false?

    _____

/20

★ **DID YOU KNOW?**

Michelangelo created some of the world's greatest marble sculptures, but he was also known as a talented painter, architect and poet in his time.

INTERNET CHALLENGES

O Write a time line of important events in Michelangelo's life.

O View pictures of the statue of David.

O View pictures of at least one other of Michelangelo's creations.

O Write some facts about Michelangelo's childhood.

PRIMARY QUIZ 15 – TEACHERS NOTES

BEFORE THE QUIZ

Vocabulary
*   Define the words 'abbreviated', 'suffix' and 'prefix'.

Suggested resources
*   Internet, atlas, chart of the human skeleton

ANSWERS

1. 9
2. true
3. cheese
4. 1523
5. govt
6. Germany
7. horseracing
8. 4 cm
9. George Eastman
10. yes

11. Mark Twain
12. end
13. around
14. Ghost
15. tuba (a)
16. temperature
17. carving knife
18. phony
19. chest
20. Poland

FURTHER EXPLORATION

Question 2 Research to find out which are the world's deadliest snakes. Find out what you should do if you are bitten by one of them.

Question 9 Compare how a digital camera works to a camera that uses film.

Question 10 If possible, obtain some carnivorous plants for the classroom and ask pupils to write observations of them.

Question 13 List some common prefixes and ask pupils to write words beginning with them.

Question 16 Invite a scientist to speak to the class about global warming.

Primary quiz 15

1. What number is multiplied by 6 to make 54?

2. A snake has to swallow things whole because it cannot chew. True or false?

3. Edam is a type of what from Holland?

4. Magellan completed his expedition to be the first to sail around the world in 1523, 1542, or 1568?

5. Write the abbreviated form of the word 'government'.

6. In which country were the Adidas and Puma footwear companies founded?

7. In which sport do the first three placegetters need to 'weigh in?'

8. If the volume of a brick is 400 cubic cm, the length 20 cm and the depth 5 cm, how wide is the brick?

9. Was the Kodak camera invented by George Kodak, George Stephenson or George Eastman?

10. Is the Venus fly trap carnivorous?

11. Who was the creator of Huckleberry Finn and Tom Sawyer?

12. Is a suffix attached to the beginning or end of a word?

13. What, beginning with 'a', is the meaning of the prefix 'circum'?

14. One of the five major festivals of Chinese culture is the Festival of the Hungry what?

15. The lowest pitched instrument of the brass family is the:
(a) tuba   (b) baritone   (c) trombone

16. Global warming is the increase in the average ... of the earth.

17. What did the farmer's wife use to cut the tails off the blind mice?

18. Someone who is not genuine is often called a ph...

19. Will you find the sternum in the knee, wrist or chest?

20. Warsaw is the capital city of ...

/20

★ **DID YOU KNOW?**

Magellan was a Portuguese explorer who became the first European to discover the Straits of Magellan and the Philippines.

INTERNET CHALLENGES

O Find a portrait of Magellan.
O Write a time line of important events in Magellan's life.
O Find out some facts about what Portugal was like during Magellan's life.

PRIMARY QUIZ 16 – TEACHERS NOTES

BEFORE THE QUIZ

Vocabulary
* Define the words 'extinct' and 'philosopher'.
* Teachers may like to pronounce the words 'insulin', 'diabetes', 'Confucius' and 'samurai' for pupils.

Suggested resources
* atlas, Internet

ANSWERS

1. 25%
2. fat
3. steel
4. dodo
5. no
6. 40s
7. boxer
8. 2.5 degrees
9. 1922
10. flora
11. Chinese
12. 1 December
13. false
14. Japan
15. singer
16. no
17. Stevenson
18. state (of USA)
19. nerve
20. Denmark

FURTHER EXPLORATION

Question 2   Read about the adaptations of camels and other desert animals and design a 'perfect' desert animal.

Question 11   Find some Confucius sayings on the Internet. Write them using calligraphy and display in the classroom. Pupils could then try writing their own 'wise' sayings.

Question 13   Create a list of interesting idioms that pupils could use in creative writing. Ask them to make up their own.

Question 17   Create a pirate character and write a narrative about his/her adventures.

Question 19   Research to find out why our funny bone hurts when we hit it, why our foot can fall asleep, why we hiccup etc.

Primary quiz 16

1. What percentage is equivalent to a quarter?

2. What is stored in a camel's hump?

3. Which is not a natural resource – iron, nickel, steel or copper?

4. In the 1860s the bird 'the ...' became extinct.

5. Is the apostrophe in the correct place in this sentence?
'Neil Armstrongs' footprints.'

6. In which decade did World War II end?

7. George Foreman made his name as a champion ...

8. If a child's maximum temperature while he was sick was 39 degrees C, and it eventually came down to 36.5 degrees C, what was the temperature range?

9. Was insulin first used in the treatment of diabetes in 1922, 1952 or 1982?

10. Complete this phrase – '... and fauna'.

11. Confucius was a great Japanese, Chinese or Persian philosopher?

12. What is the first day of summer in the southern hemisphere?

13. To 'get into hot water' means you have done a good turn. True or false?

14. Where was a samurai warrior's homeland?

15. Was Frank Sinatra a famous singer, painter or artist?

16. Do nuclear power stations, in working condition, create air pollution?

17. The character Long John Silver was created by Robert Louis ...

18. Is Alaska a city, state or country?

19. The 'funny bone' isn't a bone, it is actually a ...

20. Which country is a Dane a native of?

/20

★ **DID YOU KNOW?**

Samurai warriors are known for fighting with swords, but they also used other weapons, such as bows and arrows and spears.

INTERNET CHALLENGES

O Find a picture of samurai armour.
O Write some of the beliefs of the samurai.
O Find the names of some famous samurai warriors and their achievements.
O What do you think life as a samurai would have been like?

PRIMARY QUIZ 17 – TEACHERS NOTES

BEFORE THE QUIZ

Suggested resources

• Internet, atlas

ANSWERS

1. 12
2. falcon
3. komodo
4. 7
5. discipline
6. true
7. Japan
8. 4
9. morse code
10. Japan
11. Scotland
12. XX
13. knives
14. Australians
15. true
16. moisture
17. puppy dog tails
18. wear
19. O
20. false

FURTHER EXPLORATION

Question 2   Write a list of animal 'speed' records; e.g. fastest runner, fastest swimmer.

Question 8   Make a range of different kites during art lessons and test fly them.

Question 9   Learn morse code and tap or write messages to a partner. Pupils could try writing their own 'secret' codes.

Question 12   Complete number problems involving Roman numerals.

Question 20   Use the Internet to find details of adventure activities you can do when visiting New Zealand.

Primary quiz 17

1. What is the highest common factor of 24 and 36?

2. The world's fastest bird is the Peregrine *f*...

3. Which 'dragon' is the world's largest lizard?

4. In 1986, the space shuttle *Challenger* exploded on take off, killing how many crew?

5. Which is the correct spelling? disipline, discipline, disciplin.

6. The human body has more than 500 muscles. True or false?

7. Sumo wrestling is the national sport of which country?

8. How many sides does a kite have?

9. What did Samuel Morse invent?

10. From which country does the traditional method of 'bonsai' (bon = bowl + sai = to plant) originate?

11. Macbeth was a fine leader of which country, starting with an S?

12. Complete this sum, then answer in Roman Numerals: IX + XI = ...

13. Write the plural of the word 'knife'.

14. Which people are known to put 'shrimps on the barbie'?

15. When painting, a piece of bread can be used as a substitute for an eraser. True or false?

16. Humidity is the measure of the amount of ... in the air.

17. What are little boys made of besides frogs and snails?

18. Would you eat, wear or throw a 'sarong?'

19. Which is the most common blood group – A, B, AB or O?

20. The north island of New Zealand is in the northern hemisphere. True or false?

/20

★ DID YOU KNOW?

The space shuttle *Challenger* had been on nine successful missions before the 1986 disaster. One of the passengers who was killed on that day was Sharon Christa McAuliffe, a teacher who had been selected from thousands of applicants to be part of a new programme called the 'Teacher in Space' programme.

INTERNET CHALLENGES

O Find out what the aim of the final *Challenger* mission was.

O There were many problems in the days leading up to the *Challenger* launch. Find out what some of them were.

O Find out the reason why the *Challenger* exploded.

O Visit the NASA website to find out what space missions will be happening in the near future.

PRIMARY QUIZ 18 – TEACHERS NOTES

BEFORE THE QUIZ

Vocabulary

• Define the words 'noun' and 'acronym'.

• Teachers may like to pronounce the words 'Auld Lang Syne', 'perennial', 'Oktoberfest', 'Yuri Gagarin' and 'Fujiyama' for pupils.

Suggested resources

• atlas, Internet

ANSWERS

1. 60
2. gorilla
3. no
4. 1768
5. believe
6. New Year's Eve
7. false
8. 300
9. DOS
10. false
11. Teresa
12. 16
13. quarter
14. Germany
15. Clark Gable
16. eco
17. false
18. Yuri Gagarin
19. knee
20. Japan

FURTHER EXPLORATION

Question 3 Use an atlas to find out which countries are closest to the Equator. What type of climate do these countries have?

Question 11 Write a biography of Mother Teresa.

Question 12 Learn to play chess in class.

Question 17 Read books written by C S Lewis and write character profiles.

Question 20 Write facts about the highest mountains in the world.

Primary quiz 18

1. What is 300 divided by 5?

2. What is the biggest great ape?

3. Does the Equator pass through China?

4. Captain James Cook made his first voyage in 1687, 1768, or 1847?

5. Which is not a noun – parrot, believe, fairy, scientist?

6. *Auld Lang Syne* is usually sung on what day?

7. Hurling and lacrosse both use sticks with a net. True or false?

8. How many years in three centuries?

9. Which of these acronyms are you most likely to see when using a computer program – DOG, DOP or DOS?

10. A perennial usually flowers once then dies. True or false?

11. Mother ... was an outstanding worker for the poor in India.

12. How many pawns are on the board at the start of a chess game?

13. Which is the second in alphabetical order? quarter, quartet, quarrel

14. 'Oktoberfest' is a well known festival of which country?

15. Which of these was not a 'screen siren' – Greta Garbo, Clark Gable, Marilyn Monroe or Jean Harlow?

16. A community of living and nonliving things that affect each other is called an ... system.

17. C S Lewis wrote the *Goosebumps* series of books. True or false?

18. Who was the first man in space – Yuri Gagarin or Buzz Aldrin?

19. The patella is more commonly known as the ... cap.

20. You can see Mount Fujiyama in which country?

/20

★ **DID YOU KNOW?**
Chess is generally believed to have been invented in India in the seventh century AD. It was designed to demonstrate and practise moves made by the army.

INTERNET CHALLENGES
O View pictures of early and modern chessboards.
O Write the names of some famous chess masters.
O Find a website that allows you to play chess online.

PRIMARY QUIZ 19 – TEACHERS NOTES

BEFORE THE QUIZ

Vocabulary

• Ensure pupils understand the term 'comparative form'.

• Teachers may like to pronounce the words 'echolocation', 'cumulonimbus', 'sarsaparilla' and 'gluteus' for pupils.

Suggested resources

• atlas, Internet

ANSWERS

1. 20
2. dolphins/bats
3. clouds
4. false
5. forty
6. 240
7. curling
8. yes
9. razor blades (disposable)
10. roots
11. Viking
12. Stone Age
13. smaller
14. Japan
15. Beethoven
16. lead
17. Jules Verne
18. paper
19. maximus
20. Sahara

FURTHER EXPLORATION

Question 3   Learn to identify different types of clouds and why they form.

Question 10   Write an explanation of how soft drinks are made.

Question 11   Research and write a report on the daily lives of the Vikings.

Question 15   Listen to some of Beethoven's music as a stimulus during creative writing sessions.

Question 18   Learn to make origami designs.

Primary quiz 19

1. What is the sum of 18 and 2?

2. 'Echolocation' is a term usually associated with which animals?

3. What is the term 'cumulonimbus' associated with?

4. George Washington became the first president of the USA in 1889. True or false?

5. Spell the next number in this series. ten, twenty, thirty, …

6. The Roman numeral CCXL represents how much?

7. Which sport played on ice uses brooms, rocks and sliders?

8. Will a tablecloth 2 metres x 3 metres fit onto a table of 5.5 square metres?

9. What did King Camp Gillette invent?

10. Sarsaparilla, the drink, is prepared from the … of the sarsaparilla plant.

11. Leif Ericsson, son of Eric the Red, was a famous *V*…

12. Which of these was the earliest – the Stone Age or Bronze Age?

13. What is the comparative form of 'small'?

14. In which country do people travel on the original 'bullet' train?

15. Complete this great musician's name – Ludwig van …

16. …–free petrol has been introduced to reduce air pollution.

17. Who wrote both *20 000 Leagues Under the Sea* and *Around the World in Eighty Days*?

18. If 'ori' means fold in Japanese, what do you think 'gami' means?

19. The body's biggest muscle is called the gluteus m…

20. Name the world's largest hot desert, that stretches across North Africa.

/20

★ **DID YOU KNOW?**

The capital of the USA, Washington DC, was named after George Washington, but he never actually lived there. While he was president, New York and then Philadelphia were the capitals.

INTERNET CHALLENGES

O Write the names of some other presidents of the USA and list their achievements.
O Write some fascinating facts about George Washington.
O Find a portrait of George Washington.

PRIMARY QUIZ 20 – TEACHERS NOTES

BEFORE THE QUIZ

Vocabulary

*   Define the words 'vertices', 'noun' and 'plural'.
*   Teachers may like to pronounce the words 'poinciana' and 'Exxon Valdez' for pupils.

Suggested resources

*   Internet

ANSWERS

1. 23
2. sloth
3. $\frac{1}{2}$ of 130
4. 1846
5. stationary
6. carbon
7. eagle
8. 8
9. yes
10. red/orange
11. JFK
12. Monkey
13. dice
14. Spanish
15. Garland
16. oil
17. curds and whey
18. drake
19. soles/palms
20. Venice

FURTHER EXPLORATION

Question 2   Compile a fact file about the sloth.

Question 9   Investigate fingerprints in the classroom. Pupils could use their fingerprints to make designs.

Question 13   Play dice games involving number during maths lessons.

Question 15   Consider the question 'If you could meet the Wizard of Oz, what would you ask for?'

Question 20   Use the Internet to plan a holiday to Venice – find a flight, some accommodation and a 'sight-seeing' activity.

Primary quiz 20

1. Increase 11 by 12.

_____

2. Rhyming with 'froth', what is the slowest moving mammal?

_____

3. Which is more – $\frac{1}{2}$ of 130 or $\frac{2}{3}$ of 90?

_____

4. A potato famine in Ireland caused millions to die or emigrate in 1256, 1546 or 1846?

_____

5. Which word is not a noun?   station, stationary, stationery

_____

6. Dry ice is simply frozen … dioxide.

_____

7. In golf, a score of three on a par five is called an …

_____

8. How many vertices does a cube have?

_____

9. Was the fingerprint system introduced before WWI?

_____

10. Which colour do you associate with the poinciana tree in bloom?

_____

11. John Kennedy, the youngest president of the USA, was widely referred to by what other 'name'?

_____

12. Most of 2004 is the Chinese Year of the Horse, Monkey or Snake?

_____

13. What is the plural form of 'die'?

_____

14. Flamenco dancing is a cultural tradition of which people?

_____

15. Judy … played Dorothy in the film *The Wizard of Oz.*

_____

16. In 1989, the ship *Exxon Valdez* ran aground near Alaska. An environmental disaster occurred because the ship spilt what?

_____

17. What was little Miss Muffet eating while she sat on her tuffet?

_____

18. What is a male duck called?

_____

19. Where on the human body is the skin the thickest?

_____

20. Which city is famous for its palaces, gondolas and canals?

_____

/20

INTERNET CHALLENGES

O Find out which animal is supposed to influence your personality, according to the Chinese calendar. Write some character traits you are supposed to have.

O Find out why there are 12 animals in the Chinese calendar. Write their names.

O Compare your Chinese animal sign to your zodiac sign. Do the personality traits for both have any similarities?

PRIMARY QUIZ 21 – TEACHERS NOTES

BEFORE THE QUIZ

Vocabulary
- Define the words 'symmetry', 'equilateral', 'abbreviation' and 'anagram'.

Suggested resources
- Internet, atlas, chart of the human body

ANSWERS

1. 3
2. ostrich
3. Thursday
4. graph
5. capital letter
6. John Lennon
7. sting like a bee
8. 3
9. heart
10. yes

11. Ronald Reagan
12. 13
13. stain
14. (c)
15. Pop
16. Group of 7
17. Enid Blyton
18. recession
19. heart
20. true

FURTHER EXPLORATION

Question 3	Read Norse legends and try writing your own.
Question 5	Write a range of different poems; e.g. haiku, cinquains etc.
Question 13	Create puzzles using anagrams.
Question 14	Ask guest speakers to talk about their favourite religious occasions.
Question 19	Learn how the heart works.

Primary quiz 21

1. What is the lowest common factor of 18 and 33?

2. Which bird is the world's fastest two-legged runner?

3. Which day of the week is named after the Norse god, Thor?

4. To the delight of music lovers around the world, Thomas Edison invented the **phono**... in 1879.

5. In poetry, the first word in each line often begins with what?

6. Who married Yoko Ono in 1969?

7. Complete this Mohammed Ali jingle, '*Float like a butterfly, ...*'.

8. How many lines of symmetry does an equilateral triangle have?

9. Which type of organ transplant did Dr Christiaan Barnard first perform in 1967?

10. Can a cactus produce flowers?

11. Which Hollywood actor later became President of the USA?

12. How many in a 'baker's dozen'?

13. Give an anagram of the word 'satin'.

14. Fasting during daylight hours through a period called Ramadan is a special time for:
(a) Buddhists (b) Hindus (c) Muslims

15. A style which emerged in the late 1950s and early 1960s was called 'P... Art'. An artist named Andy Warhol was one to make his mark in this area.

16. What does the abbreviation G-7 stand for?

17. Who created the 'Famous Five'?

18. Beginning with 'R', what is the term for an economic downturn?

19. Where in the body will you find the left ventricle?

20. The capital city of the country of Singapore is Singapore. True or false?

★ **DID YOU KNOW?**

A cactus has thin spines for two reasons. If it had large leaves, it would lose too much water in the harsh desert conditions in which it lives. The spines also discourage animals from attacking it in an attempt to get water from its fleshy leaves.

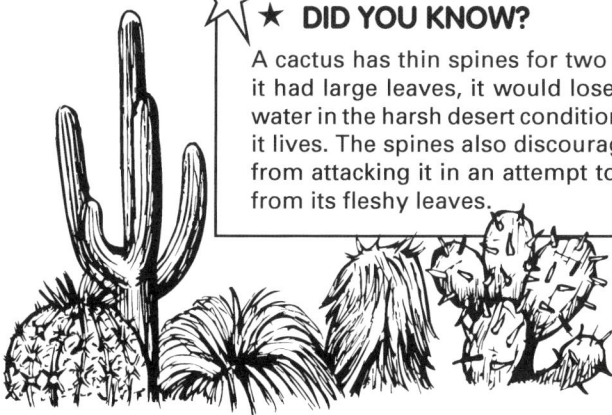

/20

INTERNET CHALLENGES

O Find pictures of some unusual cactuses.

O In which countries will you find native cactuses growing?

O Write a list of fascinating facts about the cactus.

O Find out how high the largest cactus can grow to.

PRIMARY QUIZ 22 – TEACHERS NOTES

BEFORE THE QUIZ

Vocabulary

* Ensure pupils understand the words 'equilateral', 'epidemic' and 'abdicated'.
* Teachers may like to pronounce the words 'tsunami', 'Angkor Wat', 'Tunisia' and 'Luxembourg' for pupils.

Suggested resources

* Internet, atlas, chart of the human skeleton

ANSWERS

1. 24
2. grasshoppers
3. wave
4. false
5. sleigh
6. failure
7. no
8. 60 degrees
9. 1980s
10. mahogany
11. VIII
12. Cambodia
13. kid
14. cous
15. tenor
16. (b)
17. upstairs/downstairs/through the town
18. both
19. yes
20. 66/67

FURTHER EXPLORATION

Question 3	Research to find out why tsunamis occur.
Question 11	Choose a king or queen of England and write a list of facts about his/her life.
Question 13	Learn the unusual names the young of some animals have.
Question 14	Find some African recipes on the Internet and try making some for a class party.
Question 17	Write your own nursery rhymes, suitable for young children.

Primary quiz 22

1. What number needs to be divided by 4 to equal 6?

   _____

2. What are locusts?

   _____

3. If 'tsu' in Japanese means 'port', what might 'nami' mean?

   _____

4. The Eiffel Tower was designed for a Paris exhibition in 1949. True or false?

   _____

5. What is the correct spelling for what Santa rides in?

   _____

6. Is a 'fiasco' a complete success or failure?

   _____

7. Is there such a thing as a left-handed hockey stick?

   _____

8. What is the size of each angle in an equilateral triangle?

   _____

9. Did AIDS reach epidemic proportions in the 1970s, 80s or 90s?

   _____

10. Unjumble this word, which is the name of a valuable reddish-brown wood – AMANYHOG.

    _____

11. The King of England at the time, Edward ..., abdicated from the throne because he fell in love with an American divorcee.

    _____

12. In which country would you find Angkor Wat?

    _____

13. What is the young of a goat called?

    _____

14. The people of North African countries such as Tunisia eat a meal called cous-...

    _____

15. The highest male singing voice is called a *t*...

    _____

16. Americans make up 5% of the world's population but consume:
    (a) 25%   (b) 35%   (c) 45%
    of the world's resources.

    _____

17. Where did Wee Willie Winkie run in his nightgown?

    _____

18. Is Luxembourg a city, a country or both?

    _____

19. If you broke your tibia bone, are you likely to need crutches?

    _____

20. How many degrees north of the equator is the Arctic Circle?

    _____

★ **DID YOU KNOW?**

The Eiffel Tower was built to commemorate the French Revolution. It is 320 metres high, including the TV antenna at the top. The public are allowed on three of the tower's levels.

INTERNET CHALLENGES

O Find pictures showing the construction of the Eiffel Tower.

O Find a website for tourists intending to visit Paris and write a list of attractions you might like to see.

O Read some fascinating facts about the Eiffel Tower.

O Find out who the Eiffel Tower was named after and why.

/20

PRIMARY QUIZ 23 – TEACHERS NOTES

BEFORE THE QUIZ

Vocabulary

*   Define the words 'abbreviation', 'pseudonym' and 'icon'.
*   Teachers may like to pronounce the words 'Evita', 'pseudonym', 'umbilical' and 'placenta' for pupils.

Suggested resources

*   Internet, atlas

ANSWERS

1. 13.2
2. gaggle
3. virus
4. South Pole
5. threw
6. Moscow
7. badminton
8. 270 mL
9. 1931
10. ponics

11. Peron
12. 27
13. shrieked
14. false
15. Twain
16. 1961
17. Anne Frank
18. Fleece
19. jugular
20. Antarctica

FURTHER EXPLORATION

Question 11	Write a time line of events in the life of Evita.
Question 15	Research to find out what Mark Twain wrote. Role play some scenes from his books.
Question 16	Consider the question 'If you were to start your own group that worked to protect animals, what would you call it and what would the group do?'
Question 17	Read parts of Anne Frank's diary. Describe how you think it would have felt to have been in her situation.
Question 18	Read a variety of Greek and Roman myths and legends. Rewrite some of them into playscripts.

Primary quiz 23

1. What is 1.32 x 10 equal to?

2. Is it a litter of geese or a gaggle of geese?

3. What does the 'V' stand for in the abbreviation HIV?

4. A tragic ending occurred when Captain Scott and his team of explorers died after reaching the ...

5. Complete the following – Today I throw, yesterday I ...

6. In which city could I visit Red Square?

7. Unjumble this to make a sport that uses a racket – MANBITDON

8. If a milk carton measured 750 millilitres, how much milk has been displaced if it now measures 480 millilitres?

9. In what year was the Empire State Building finished – 1931, 1951, or 1971?

10. The method of growing plants in gravel etc. and having nutrient-enriched water pumped through it, is known as *hydro*...

11. Madonna played the lead role in a film called *Evita*. What was Evita's surname?

12. XXVII is a Roman numeral for which number?

13. Which word describes the loudest sound? whispered, talked, shrieked

14. The Fiat is a French icon. True or false?

15. A pseudonym was used by Samuel Clements, who for the purposes of his writing, wished to be known as Mark ...

16. Was the WWF (then World Wildlife Fund) first launched in 1942, 1961 or 1986?

17. Who wrote a now famous diary of her time while in hiding in Amsterdam during World War II?

18. Jason and the Argonauts searched for the Golden ...

19. Which word is unlikely to be used in childbirth – umbilical, placenta, or jugular?

20. On which continent is Mt Vinson Massif the highest mountain?

★ **DID YOU KNOW?**

The giant panda, an endangered species, is the logo of the WWF. The WWF helps to protect animals and environments from around the world.

INTERNET CHALLENGES

O Visit the website of the WWF and find out about some of their latest projects.

O Find out the names of some animals that are endangered.

O Find the websites of some other groups that help to protect animals or environments.

/20

PRIMARY QUIZ 24 – TEACHERS NOTES

BEFORE THE QUIZ

Vocabulary
- Define the words 'icon', 'anagram' and 'suffix'.
- Teachers may like to pronounce the words 'edelweiss' and 'Bjorn Borg' for pupils.

Suggested resources
- Internet, atlas

ANSWERS

1. £3.00
2. (Siberian) tiger
3. false
4. 1912
5. easily
6. dire
7. 9
8. 2.645 kg
9. false
10. *The Sound of Music*

11. Owens
12. (a)
13. review
14. wooden clogs
15. Wayne
16. people
17. fiddle
18. bug
19. incisor
20. false

FURTHER EXPLORATION

Question 4   Read eyewitness accounts of the sinking of the *Titanic* and write your own impression of what it might have been like to witness this event.

Question 9   Write a list of Einstein's achievements.

Question 10   Explain which is your favourite film musical and why.

Question 13   Expand spelling words being studied in class.

Question 18   Learn about some dance crazes of the past and try them out in small groups.

Primary quiz 24

1. If €1.00 is worth £0.60, how many pounds will five euro be worth?

2. What is the biggest species of cat?

3. The population of Australia is just over three million. True or false?

4. The *Titanic* sank on its maiden voyage in 1912, 1913 or 1915?

5. Spell the combination of 'easy' + 'ly'

6. Give an anagram of word 'ride'.

7. To win in squash you need to score ... points (with an advantage of 2).

8. What is 2645 g expressed in kilograms?

9. Albert Einstein invented the hovercraft. True or false?

10. A song about the alpine flowering plant 'edelweiss' was made famous in which film starring Julie Andrews?

★ **DID YOU KNOW?**

The wreck of the *Titanic* was discovered in 1986, resting 13 000 feet below the surface of the ocean. Some of its contents were still intact, including porcelain dishes and bottles of wine!

11. One of the truly great Olympic champions was Jessie ..., a USA sprinter who won four gold medals at the 1936 Berlin Games.

12. A spirit level tells if things:
    (a) are horizontal
    (b) contain alcohol
    (c) are underground

13. Which word does not use the suffix 'sion'? persuade, revise, review

14. Which is not a Swedish icon – Abba, wooden clogs, Bjorn Borg, or Volvo?

15. Born Marion Morrison, actor John ... changed his name when it appeared he would find it tough getting roles such as a tough talking cowboy.

16. Wildscapes are where nature still dominates, but townscapes are where ... dominate.

17. What was the cat playing when he saw the cow jump over the moon?

18. A popular 1930s/1940s dance was called the *Jitter*...

19. Unjumble this to make a word which is a type of tooth – SCOINIR.

20. The Tropic of Cancer passes through the United States of America. True or false?

INTERNET CHALLENGES
O View pictures of the *Titanic* and its memorabilia.
O Read passenger accounts of the sinking.
O Find out the numbers of survivors from each passenger class.
O Read about why the *Titanic* sank and why so many people perished.

/20

PRIMARY QUIZ 25 – TEACHERS NOTES

BEFORE THE QUIZ

Vocabulary
- Define the word 'adverb'.
- Teachers may like to pronounce the words 'Rudyard' and 'Scandinavian' for pupils.

Suggested resources
- Internet, atlas

ANSWERS

1. 130
2. gorilla
3. Sunday
4. prohibition
5. quickly
6. second
7. volleyball
8. 6
9. astronomy
10. red
11. Hendrix
12. *Machines*
13. hearth
14. Russian
15. wall
16. four
17. snake
18. Norway
19. liver
20. Rio Grande

FURTHER EXPLORATION

Question 2 Write a list of characteristics all primates have.

Question 6 Find out why clocks were wound back on this date.

Question 14 Read about some wedding traditions from around the world.

Question 15 Paint a class mural.

Question 17 Write your own 'just so' story after reading some of Kipling's.

Primary quiz 25

1. What is double 65?

2. Which is the biggest primate?

3. If 5 May is a Saturday, what is 20 May?

4. In 1920 the USA government passed a law banning alcohol. This became known as the *Pro*... era.

5. Which is the adverb – quickly, fierce, cheerful, plump?

6. On 1 July 1983, clocks were put back by one ...

7. In which sport will you hear the terms 'digs', 'kills' and 'aces'?

8. How many sides does a hexagon have?

9. What is known as the 'science of the heavens'?

10. What colour berries (when ripe) can be found on a holly tree?

11. The great left-handed guitarist, Jimi ..., died in 1970, aged 27.

12. Complete this movie film – *Those Magnificent Men in Their Flying ...*

13. Which is the odd one out? hearth, earth, pearl, learnt

14. To break champagne glasses at a *R*... wedding ceremony is a good sign – the more you break, the happier the marriage will be.

15. A mural is a decorative painting which is applied directly to a ...

16. The fraction of the world's population which live in China is one in every ...

17. What kind of animal was Kaa in Rudyard Kipling's novel *The Jungle Book*?

18. The name of which Scandinavian country means 'the northern way'?

19. Which body part, starting with 'l', breaks up the fats you eat?

20. Which river forms part of the border between Mexico and the USA?

/20

★ **DID YOU KNOW?**

Rudyard Kipling's *The Jungle Book* and *Just So Stories* are both considered children's classics. Some of the Just So stories you might know include 'How the Camel Got His Hump' and 'How the Leopard Got His Spots'.

INTERNET CHALLENGES

O Find out some facts about Rudyard Kipling's life.

O When did Kipling write *The Jungle Book* and *Just So Stories*?

O Write a list of three other books or poems Kipling wrote.

O Find out some facts about the animated film based on *The Jungle Book*.

PRIMARY QUIZ 26 – TEACHERS NOTES

BEFORE THE QUIZ

Vocabulary
- Define the words 'squared', 'superlative' and 'conjunction'.
- Teachers may like to pronounce the words 'pneumatic', 'toreador', 'Rastafarianism' and 'Serengeti' for pupils.

Suggested resources
- Internet, atlas

ANSWERS

1. 64
2. koala
3. died
4. true
5. as/because
6. *Bang*
7. bullfighter
8. 22.30 hours
9. electromagnetic
10. cotton
11. *Millionaire*
12. Netherlands
13. best
14. Jamaica
15. 4
16. Tanzania
17. sleeping
18. 23
19. circulatory
20. Mediterranean

FURTHER EXPLORATION

Question 7	Prepare a campaign that protests against or gives support to bullfighting.
Question 15	Invite members of an orchestra to visit the class and explain what their daily life is like.
Question 16	Describe which national park you would most like to visit and why.
Question 18	Write a letter or an email to a sportsperson you admire.
Question 20	Design an island you would like to spend a holiday on.

Primary quiz 26

1. What is 8 squared?

2. Unjumble this to find the name of an Australian animal – LOAKA.

3. A widower is a man whose wife has …?

4. The Wall Street stock market collapse of 1929 led to the Great Depression. True or false?

5. 'He is sad. His dog is missing.' Add the best conjunction.

6. Complete this film title – *Chitty, Chitty, Bang, …*?

7. What is a toreador?

8. Write 10.30 p.m. in 24-hour format.

9. Are radio waves electromagnetic or pneumatic?

10. Kapok is a fluffy material which is used for stuffing furniture. It comes from the silk *c*… tree.

11. Lauren Bacall, Marilyn Monroe and Betty Grable all starred in a film called *How to Marry a …*

12. In which country is the city of Amsterdam?

13. What is the superlative form of 'good'?

14. Rastafarianism is a faith that has its origins on which Caribbean island?

15. A symphony is a large scale orchestral work, usually in … movements.

16. One of the world's finest national parks is the Serengeti in T… in East Africa.

17. What was Little Boy Blue doing under the haystack?

18. Which number shirt has been worn by both Michael Jordan and David Beckham?

19. Is the heart a part of the respiratory or circulatory systems?

20. Malta, Sicily and Crete are all islands in the … Sea.

/20

★ **DID YOU KNOW?**

Amsterdam's major tourist attractions are found in its 'canal belt' – concentric canals that radiate out from the city centre.

INTERNET CHALLENGES

O Find a map of Amsterdam.

O Write a list of the major tourist attractions of the country Amsterdam is found in.

O Find the different types of musical instruments in a symphony orchestra.

O Visit the Anne Frank Foundation website and find out about her life in Amsterdam.

PRIMARY QUIZ 27 – TEACHERS NOTES

BEFORE THE QUIZ

Vocabulary
- Define the words 'adverb', 'verb', 'adjective' and 'anagram'.
- Teachers may like to pronounce the words 'Chihuahua', 'Comaneci', 'durian', 'baht' and 'euphemism' for pupils.

Suggested resources
- Internet, atlas, chart of the human skeleton

ANSWERS

1. 52
2. true
3. *Lights*
4. Australia
5. adverb
6. Antarctica
7. 8
8. 180
9. Einstein
10. false
11. 10
12. smell/taste
13. sword
14. Thailand
15. pleasant
16. Mauritius
17. *Wind in the Willows*
18. *Rollercoaster*
19. sternum
20. east

FURTHER EXPLORATION

Question 2	Research different dog breeds on the Internet and find out what purposes they were originally bred for.
Question 4	Invite an airline pilot to talk to the class about his/her job.
Question 6	Find out what the climate is like in Antarctica.
Question 11	Visit a website that explains what is involved in gymnastics training for someone your age who is aiming for the Olympic Games.
Question 15	Explore euphemisms for different aspects of life; e.g. death, getting older, getting married.

Primary quiz 27

1. What number do I need to add to 48 to reach 100?

2. The chihuahua is the smallest breed of dog. True or false?

3. Complete the book title – *The Northern ...*

4. In 1920, Amy Johnson flew solo from London to ...

5. Is the bold word an adverb, verb or adjective? '*The elephant trumpeted **loudly** to its herd.*'

6. If you were living at Mawson Station, where would you be?

7. How many players are left at the quarterfinals stage of a tournament?

8. How many degrees = a straight line?

9. Who can the equation $E = mc^2$ be attributed to?

10. The leaves of a giant water lily can grow to four metres across. True or false?

11. Nadia Comaneci was the first woman in Olympic gymnastics history to score a ...

12. Durian is a fruit found in several Asian countries. It is easily recognised by its disgusting (to many people) ...

13. Give an anagram of the word WORDS.

14. If I was using 'baht' to buy something, which country would I be in?

15. A 'euphemism' is a polite or inoffensive way of saying something **un**...

16. On which island in the Indian Ocean did the dodo live until its extinction in 1861?

17. In which book can you read about Toad Hall?

18. Complete this Ronan Keating song title – *Life is a ...*

19. Which is not an arm bone – humerus, radius, sternum, or ulna?

20. Is Kenya on the west or east coast of Africa?

/20

★ **DID YOU KNOW?**

The dodo was a flightless pigeon about the size of a swan. Its extinction, caused by the arrival of Europeans to its home, has given rise to the saying 'dead as a dodo'.

INTERNET CHALLENGES

O Find how Europeans caused the extinction of the dodo.

O Read some eyewitness accounts of the dodo.

O View some pictures of the dodo.

O Write a list of other flightless birds found around the world.

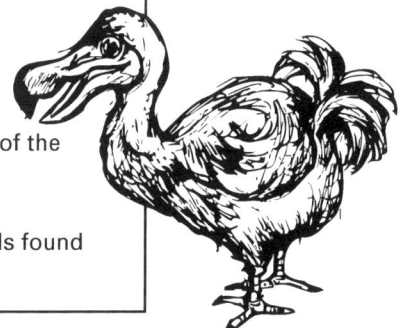

PRIMARY QUIZ 28 – TEACHERS NOTES

BEFORE THE QUIZ

Vocabulary

* Teachers may like to pronounce the words 'proboscis', 'Virunga' and 'Zaire' for pupils.

Suggested resources

* atlas, Internet

ANSWERS

1. 4.36
2. nose
3. wicketkeeper
4. Watergate
5. full/filled/crowded
6. Philip Pullman
7. surfing
8. 6 sq m
9. 19th
10. (c)
11. Pelé
12. blowfish/puffer
13. fortune
14. *Greek*
15. Queen Elizabeth II
16. hippopotamus
17. a pig
18. Ness
19. socket
20. diamonds

FURTHER EXPLORATION

Question 3   Write a biography of a famous cricketer.

Question 6   Read *The Northern Lights* from Philip Pullman's 'Dark Materials' trilogy.

Question 7   Sort sports terms into the correct sports.

Question 18   Create your own 'monster' mystery in a remote location you choose. Provide pictures, 'facts' and eyewitness accounts.

Question 20   Create a tour of South Africa that would appeal to someone of a certain age group.

Primary quiz 28

1. What is 43.6 divided by 10?

   _____

2. Does a proboscis monkey have a really long nose, tail, or ears?

   _____

3. What is the cricket equivalent of baseball's catcher?

   _____

4. What was the name of the scandal which led to the resignation of American president, Richard Nixon?

   _____

5. If something is 'jam-packed' then you can definitely say it is …

   _____

6. Who wrote 'The Subtle Knife' and 'The Amber Spyglass'?

   _____

7. In which sport will you hear the term 'goofy footer'?

   _____

8. What is the area of a cubic metre net?

   _____

9. Traffic lights were introduced into London in which century?

   _____

10. What is 'composting?'
    (a) correct way to plant seeds
    (b) the spraying of insecticides to kill pests
    (c) the rotting of both plant and animal matter

    _____

11. Who is the youngest player to score a goal in a football World Cup final (as at 2004) – David Beckham, Diego Maradona or Pelé?

    _____

12. 'Fugu' is a fish dish prepared in Japan by expert chefs. It is more commonly known as the …

    _____

13. In the word 'unfortunate', what is the root word?

    _____

14. Complete the following film title – *Zorba the …*

    _____

15. The first major international TV transmission was of the 1953 coronation of which queen?

    _____

16. The Virunga National Park in Zaire is the home to an animal with an extraordinary large mouth, known as the …

    _____

17. What did *Tom, Tom, the Piper's son* steal?

    _____

18. In which Scottish loch is there said to be a famous monster?

    _____

19. Ball and … joints allow your hips and shoulders to move in all directions.

    _____

20. South Africa is very rich in gold and *d*…

    _____

/20

★ **DID YOU KNOW?**

Stories about a monster living in a certain Scottish loch (a lake) have been around for centuries. Eyewitness accounts describe an animal that looks like a long-necked dinosaur. No physical evidence of the animal, except for some dubious photographs, has yet been provided.

INTERNET CHALLENGES
○ Use a search engine to locate at least three websites that provide information about the monster.
○ Read some eyewitness accounts of the monster.
○ View some photographs that people claim are of the monster and write whether or not you think they are fakes.

PRIMARY QUIZ 29 – TEACHERS NOTES

BEFORE THE QUIZ

Vocabulary

- Define the words 'prime' and 'contraction'.

Suggested resources

- Internet

ANSWERS

1. 23
2. spine/backbone
3. rodent
4. 1976
5. brought
6. purple
7. one day international
8. 55 L
9. umbrella
10. balsa
11. Lady Godiva
12. true
13. you'd
14. Americans
15. upside down
16. (b) 3
17. *Black Beauty*
18. side by side
19. eye
20. Japan

FURTHER EXPLORATION

Question 3   Research an animal that protects itself using spikes or spines.

Question 9   Find out what Thomas Edison invented.

Question 12   Make healthy flavoured popcorn for a party for a younger class.

Question 14   Write a brochure that educates people about the dangers of smoking.

Question 20   Read the lyrics of some different national anthems. Write lyrics for a new national anthem for your home country.

1. What is the first prime number after 20?

2. If an animal is an invertebrate, it has no what?

3. Is a porcupine a rodent or a reptile?

4. The Concorde began its regular service in 1936, 1956 or 1976?

5. Which word is wrong in this sentence? *'Dad brought a second-hand lawn mower from the hardware store.'*

6. What colour is lavender?

7. In cricket what is a ODI?

8. What is the total capacity of 10 containers each holding 5.5 litres of water?

9. Which of these did Thomas Edison not invent – the umbrella, the phonograph or the light bulb?

10. Which of these timbers is lighter than cork – balsa, oak or bamboo?

11. Which 'Lady' supposedly rode naked through the streets of Coventry?

12. Popcorn is not a modern day invention – it used to be eaten by the Incas. True or false?

13. Write the contraction of 'you would'.

14. The cultivation of tobacco appears to have spread through various migrations of Native ...

15. In 1961, in the Museum of Modern Art in New York, a painting was hung ... and the error was not discovered for 47 days!

16. The Arabian oryx is an animal saved from extinction—just. Its numbers got down to an amazingly low:
(a) 2   (b) 3   (c) 8

17. Which Anna Sewell novel tells the life story of a black horse?

18. What is meant by walking 'abreast'?

19. REM sleep is short for Rapid ... Movement sleep.

20. *The Reign of our Emperor* is the national anthem of which country?

★ DID YOU KNOW?

The Concorde was the first civil supersonic aircraft. It could fly at 2125 kilometres per hour!

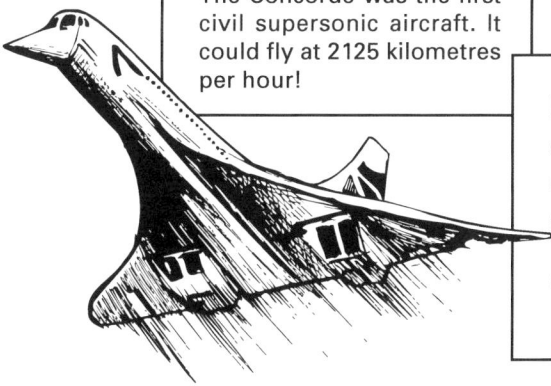

/20

INTERNET CHALLENGES
O Find out why the Concorde is no longer flying.
O Learn about supersonic flight.
O Find out what speed the fastest modern jet passenger aircraft can reach.
O View pictures of the Concorde and find out the reasons for its unusual shape.

PRIMARY QUIZ 30 – TEACHERS NOTES

BEFORE THE QUIZ

Vocabulary

- Define the words 'homophone' and 'synonym' for pupils.
- Teachers may like to pronounce the words 'chinchilla', 'Karachi', 'Kournikova', 'Geiger', 'Johann Strauss' and 'Bhutan' for pupils.

Suggested resources

- atlas, Internet

ANSWERS

1. 12
2. rodent
3. Pakistan
4. 1960s
5. dough
6. lanky
7. tennis
8. 15
9. counter
10. stigma
11. Waltz
12. Amsterdam
13. mare
14. Dutch
15. serenade
16. giant panda
17. *The Wind in the Willows*
18. higher/law
19. false
20. Nepal

FURTHER EXPLORATION

Question 5	Explore homonyms and homographs.
Question 8	Learn about the 24-hour clock and why it is important in some professions.
Question 9	Find out what a Geiger counter is used to measure.
Question 18	Hold mock trials involving characters from well-known stories who committed 'crimes'; e.g. Goldilocks – breaking and entering.
Question 20	Research to find out what equipment you would need to take to climb Mount Everest.

Primary quiz 30

1. Round 12.38 to the nearest whole number.

2. What type of an animal is a chinchilla?

3. Karachi is a major city in which country?

4. The Vietnam War took up most of which decade?

5. Spell correctly the homophone of 'doe'.

6. What synonym, beginning with 'l', means 'awkwardly thin and tall'?

7. In which sport did Anna Kournikova make her mark?

8. How many hours are there between 8 am and 11 pm?

9. In 1913, Hans Geiger invented the Geiger ...

10. Unjumble this to make a word which is a flower part – GASTIM

11. Johann Strauss Jr was known as 'The **W**... King'.

12. The city of New York was first known as New ...

13. What is the mother of a foal called? stallion, mare, cow

14. **D**... wedding couples plant 'lily-of-the-valley' in their garden so that they can renew their love every year when the plant blooms.

15. A ... might be played in the evening outside a lover's or sweetheart's window.

16. Which animal has the WWF chosen to promote its cause?

17. Which was not a major Walt Disney production – *Mickey Mouse, Pinocchio, The Wind in the Willows, The Lion King* or *Snow White and the Seven Dwarfs*?

18. A barrister is a lawyer who represent people in ... courts.

19. You feel pain in a part of the brain called the thyroid. True or false?

20. In which country is Mount Everest – Nepal, India or Bhutan?

★ **DID YOU KNOW?**

Walt Disney was responsible for the idea of Disneyland. He wanted to create a magical place where children and parents could have fun. Construction of the park began in 1954 and it opened in 1955.

/20

INTERNET CHALLENGES

O Find a map of the Disneyland park and identify the rides you would like to try.

O Find out approximately how many people have visited Disneyland.

O Find out where Disneyworld and Euro Disney are located.

O Write a time line of events in Walt Disney's life.

PRIMARY QUIZ 31 – TEACHERS NOTES

BEFORE THE QUIZ

Vocabulary

- Define the words 'homophone', 'beneficiary' and 'neurons'.
- Teachers may like to pronounce the words 'Kasparov' and 'Chernobyl' for pupils.

Suggested resources

- Internet

ANSWERS

1. 37
2. no
3. autumn
4. Pope Paul II
5. straight
6. no runs scored
7. chess
8. (a)
9. air/matter
10. node

11. Tonto
12. *Stone*
13. celebrate
14. German
15. *Mr Hyde*
16. fallout
17. Whittington
18. the lot/everything
19. motor
20. false

FURTHER EXPLORATION

Question 2	Write a list of characteristics that all marsupials have.
Question 3	View pictures of autumn leaves. Use the colours to inspire poetry writing sessions.
Question 4	Read about the life of the current Pope.
Question 14	Create a recipe for a dessert you think would be irresistible.
Question 20	Research the average monthly temperatures in Finland. Compare to the average monthly temperatures in the country you live.

Primary quiz 31

1. The difference in age between Henry (14) and Tom (51) is how much?

2. Is a tortoise a marsupial?

3. 'Fall' is the American term for which season?

4. The death of Pope Paul I occurred in 1978. His replacement was …

5. Correctly spell the homophone for 'strait'.

6. What does a 'maiden over' mean in cricket?

7. Garry Kasparov was a world champion in which sport?

8. One cubic centimetre displaces:
   (a) 1 mL   (b) 10 mL   (c) 100 mL

9. A vacuum is a space entirely empty of …

10. What, starting with 'n', is a joint along a plant stem where a leaf can grow?

11. Most have heard of the Lone Ranger, but what was his Indian companion's name – Pancho or Tonto?

12. Complete this song title by Captain Hook – *On the Cover of the Rolling* …

13. To 'kick up your heels' is a figure of speech meaning to *c*…

14. Black Forest cake is a luscious example of … cuisine.

15. Robert Louis Stevenson wrote a story after a dream. It was eventually published as *The Strange Case of Dr Jekyll and* …

16. The radioactive … from the world's worst nuclear disaster at Chernobyl in 1986 will be felt for years to come.

17. The boy who listened to the Bow Bells was Dick who?

18. A sole beneficiary of a will would expect to receive …

19. The three types of neurons are sensory, connector and *m*… neurons?

20. Finland has the highest average temperature of any country. True or false?

★ **DID YOU KNOW?**

Robert Louis Stevenson's other popular novels include *Treasure Island* (1883), *Kidnapped* (1886) and *The Master Of Ballantrae* (1889).

INTERNET CHALLENGES

O Write a timeline of events in Stevenson's life.
O Find an excerpt from *Treasure Island*.
O Read the plot outline of *Kidnapped*.

/20

PRIMARY QUIZ 32 – TEACHERS NOTES

BEFORE THE QUIZ

Vocabulary

*   Define the words 'palindrome', 'proper noun', 'common noun' and 'abbreviation'.
*   Teachers may like to pronounce the words 'dirigible', 'Bonenkai' and 'ambidextrous' for pupils.

Suggested resources

*   Internet

ANSWERS

1. 0.8
2. meerkat
3. *Alive*
4. Elvis Presley
5. capital letter
6. microchip
7. bunny/lure
8. 360°
9. fly it
10. true
11. Paris
12. Anne Frank
13. noon
14. Japan
15. Mickey Mouse
16. Amnesty International/Artificial Intelligence
17. 4 and 20 blackbirds
18. eye
19. both hands equally
20. China

FURTHER EXPLORATION

Question 4   Listen to early rock and roll music and compare it to the popular music you listen to now.

Question 9   Draw a design for a new type of flying machine.

Question 14   Research to find out about New Year customs around the world.

Question 19   Conduct a class or school survey to find out the number of right-handers, left-handers or ambidextrous people. Create a graph to display your findings.

Question 20   Write a list of country 'world records'; e.g. smallest country, most northern country.

Primary quiz 32

1. Which is the greatest amount, 75% or 0.8?

2. Unjumble this word to make the name of a creature which starred in *The Lion King* – TEMAKER.

3. Complete this Bee Gees song title – *Stayin' ...*?

4. The death of ..., 'The King,' in 1977 was mourned by millions worldwide.

5. What distinguishes a proper noun from a common noun?

6. Is a microchip, a microfilm or a microcosm made from silicon?

7. What is the term used for what greyhounds try to catch in a race?

8. The four angles of a square add up to how many degrees?

9. What would you do with a dirigible – fly it, drive it on land or steer?

10. Bamboo is the world's fastest growing plant. True or false?

11. According to Greek legend, who 'kidnapped' Helen of Troy?

12. Which author wrote *The Diary of Anne Frank*?

13. What word indicating a time of the day is a palindrome?

14. A common practice is to 'see in the New Year' but in ... they have Bonenkai parties to forget about the troubles of the past year.

15. *Steamboat Willie* was the name of the film in which the Walt Disney character ... made his debut.

16. What does the abbreviation 'AI' mean?

17. What was baked in the *Sing a Song of Sixpence* pie?

18. A cataract is a condition affecting which body part?

19. To be 'ambidextrous' means you can use what?

20. What is the world's most populous country?

/20

INTERNET CHALLENGES

O Write the names of three of the main characters from *The Lion King* and the actors who provided their voices.

O Write three fascinating facts about the making of *The Lion King*.

O Listen to a sound effect, voice or song from the film.

★ **DID YOU KNOW?**

The creators of *The Lion King* studied the movements of real lions and lion cubs and used their observations to help make the animated lion characters in the film as realistic as possible.

PRIMARY QUIZ 33 – TEACHERS NOTES

BEFORE THE QUIZ

Vocabulary

- Define the words 'abbreviation', 'continent' and 'contraction'.

Suggested resources

- Internet, atlas

ANSWERS

1. 60
2. gosling
3. Yangtze
4. 1650
5. exclamation mark
6. Attorney General
7. 7
8. yes
9. control
10. salt(s)

11. Romeo
12. Africa
13. won't
14. Jewish
15. (dis)torted
16. (c)
17. *Silver*
18. London
19. identical
20. Pacific

FURTHER EXPLORATION

Question 7	Hold a 'mini'-heptathlon where the pupils try out seven different events.
Question 10	Create a poster that gives information about the effects of salinity.
Question 15	View some Expressionist paintings on the Internet and try to paint a picture in the same style.
Question 18	Find out the significance of the clothes worn by guards like the beefeaters (Yeomen of the Guard). Design a new outfit for them.
Question 19	Write a creative narrative on what it would be like to wake up one morning and find you have an identical twin. If you already are a twin, write what it would be like to suddenly find you are a quadruplet!

Primary quiz 33

1. What is one-third of 180?

2. What is a young goose called?

3. The Ch'ang Chiang River in Asia is better known in the west as the Y...?

4. The world's population hit around 500 million in 1650, 1750 or 1850?

5. Is a question mark, full stop or exclamation mark needed in this sentence? *'What a mess ...'* Mum *remarked*.

6. What does the abbreviation 'Att. Gen.' mean?

7. How many events are there in a heptathlon?

8. Is 4.2 kg divided by 6 > 600 g?

9. What does the button abbreviated to 'ctrl' on a computer keyboard stand for?

10. Salinity refers to an excess of ... in the soil.

11. Which character from a play said *'But, soft! What light through yonder window breaks'*?

12. In which continent is the country of Gambia?

13. Write the contraction of 'will not.'

14. Which people would be celebrating Yom Kippur after ten days of penitence?

15. Expressionism was a 20th century style of painting which expressed a painters emotional feelings through **dis**... shapes and vibrant colours.

16. The most common bird that ever lived is now extinct. Was it:
    (a) the Asian Red Gull?
    (b) the South American Tern?
    (c) the North American Passenger Pigeon?

17. One of the Chronicles of Narnia is called *The ... Chair*.

18. A beefeater is a guard at the Tower of ...?

19. Do identical or non-identical twins share a placenta?

20. In which ocean is the island country of Fiji?

★ **DID YOU KNOW?**

Some pairs of identical twins can communicate in their own secret languages that no-one else can understand.

INTERNET CHALLENGES

O Write three fascinating facts about identical twins.
O Find out how common giving birth to identical twins is.
O Find an online club or society for identical twins. What do they offer?

/20

PRIMARY QUIZ 34 – TEACHERS NOTES

BEFORE THE QUIZ

Vocabulary

* Define the word 'palindrome'.
* Teachers may like to pronounce the words 'Stradavari', 'tae-kwon-do' and 'Paraguay' for pupils.

Suggested resources

* Internet, atlas, chart of the human skeleton

ANSWERS

1. 25.8
2. whale shark
3. China
4. violin
5. advertisement
6. plagiarism
7. tennis
8. 360
9. cursor
10. no
11. Noah
12. Korea
13. kayak
14. Malaysia
15. true
16. white
17. cinders
18. jellyfish
19. collar bone
20. true

FURTHER EXPLORATION

Question 4   View pictures of Stradivarius violins, violas and cellos. Find out what kinds of prices they sell for and why.

Question 8   Explore the number of degrees in different 2-D shapes.

Question 11   If you were Noah and you could only take 20 pairs of animals on the ark, which would you take?

Question 12   Compare two forms of martial arts.

Question 18   Create a wanted poster for one of Australia's deadliest animals.

Primary quiz 34

1. Round the following decimal to one decimal place – 25.783

2. What is the world's largest fish?

3. In 1908, two-year-old Pu Yi became emperor of which country?

4. In 1666, Stradavari made his first ...

5. Change 'advertise' into a noun.

6. Copying or using someone else's writings or ideas is known as **pla**...

7. Patrick Rafter won two USA Opens in golf, squash or tennis?

8. How many degrees are there in a circle?

9. Name the flashing line on a computer screen which shows where the next letter will appear.

10. Are vegetables generally a good source of energy?

11. Which biblical character made a boat out of gopher wood?

12. Does tae-kwon-do originate in Korea, Japan or neither?

13. Which word meaning 'a small canoe' is a palindrome?

14. Which country has the 'ringgit' as its unit of currency?

15. A 'prima donna' is the main female singer in an opera. True or false?

16. One of the most threatened species of rhinoceros is the ... rhinoceros. It is estimated there are fewer than 30 of them left.

17. What did Little Polly Flinders sit among?

18. What type of Australian animal is called a 'bluebottle'?

19. What is the more common term for the clavicle?

20. The South American country of Paraguay has no coastline at all. True or false?

/20

★ DID YOU KNOW?

There are fewer than 18 000 rhinoceros left. This is due to habitat loss and humans killing them for their horns. Among other things, rhino horn is used in traditional medicine in Asia.

INTERNET CHALLENGES

O Approximately how many of each species of rhinoceros is left?

O Find pictures of rhinoceroses.

O Write a list of facts about rhinos under the headings 'Diet', 'Habitat' and 'Predators'.

PRIMARY QUIZ 35 – TEACHERS NOTES

BEFORE THE QUIZ

Vocabulary
- Define the word 'homophone'.
- Teachers may like to pronounce the words 'Mir' and 'corroboree' for pupils.

Suggested resources
- Internet, atlas

ANSWERS

1. 0
2. cow (young < 3)
3. Checker
4. true
5. permanent
6. *Manger*
7. butterfly
8. 760 000 km²
9. USSR/Russia
10. carbon dioxide
11. Austen
12. salary
13. rein/reign
14. Australia
15. (cl)imax
16. Teacher check
17. purple
18. booby
19. adrenaline
20. England

FURTHER EXPLORATION

Question 4   Read some children's versions of Shakespeare plays and write your opinions of them.

Question 10   Devise a television commercial in a small group that gives public information on the importance of saving trees.

Question 11   Hold a debate on the topic 'It would have been more difficult to write a book before the computer age'.

Question 14   Create a dance that tells a story in a small group.

Question 17   Role-play scenes from the Harry Potter books.

Primary quiz 35

1. Which one of these numbers is not a whole number? 0, 1, 2, 10

2. What is a heifer?

3. Put a surname to this famous rock and roller – Chubby ...

4. William Shakespeare wrote his first play in 1590. True or false?

5. Unjumble this word, ending in 'ent'. **empnnraet**

6. Complete this Christmas carol title – *Away in a ...*

7. Which is the missing stroke in a swimming medley – freestyle, breaststroke, backstroke, ...?

8. If the approximate length of Chile is 3800 km and the approximate width is only 200 km, what will the total area be in square kilometres?

9. The space station named *Mir* was/is a project of which country?

10. What gas do plants 'breathe in'?

11. Jane ... was only 21 when she wrote *Pride and Prejudice*.

12. Spell correctly the near-homophone of 'celery'.

13. Give two homophones for the word 'rain'.

14. The original peoples of which country perform a sacred dance called a 'corroboree'?

15. A series of statements or events rising in order of intensity is known as a *cl*...

16. Does your school have a recycling programme?

17. In *Harry Potter and the Prisoner of Azkaban*, what was the colour of the Knight Bus which saved Harry?

18. Someone who comes last in a humorous contest is said to collect the ... prize.

19. What does the adrenal gland produce when you are afraid or angry?

20. The Prime Meridian passes through England, France or Switzerland?

★ **DID YOU KNOW?**

The birthplace of William Shakespeare, Stratford-upon-Avon, is one of England's most popular tourist attractions. People can visit properties associated with Shakespeare, including his birthplace. They can also watch plays performed by the Royal Shakespeare Company.

/20

INTERNET CHALLENGES

O Find some pictures of the Shakespeare properties in Stratford-upon-Avon.

O Read extracts from a Shakespeare play.

O Write a time line of events from Shakespeare's life.

O List at least three Shakespeare plays that have been made into films.

PRIMARY QUIZ 36 – TEACHERS NOTES

BEFORE THE QUIZ

Vocabulary
* Define the words 'adverb' and 'synonym'.
* Teachers may like to pronounce the words 'Canaveral', 'biennial', 'Gustav' and 'Rwanda' for pupils.

Suggested resources
* Internet, atlas

ANSWERS

1. 121
2. No
3. Iran
4. 1815
5. patiently
6. purgatory
7. yes
8. 220 km
9. NASA
10. 2 years
11. Sweden
12. 69
13. tired
14. working
15. Rin Tin Tin
16. Zaire
17. *Cupboard*
18. *Bug*
19. bronchi
20. Kenya

FURTHER EXPLORATION

Question 7	Find out details about orienteering from club websites and decide if you would like to try it.
Question 9	Visit the NASA website to find out what the latest explorations of space are.
Question 14	Research to find out about some Russian customs.
Question 17	Read *The Indian in the Cupboard* and write a book review.
Question 19	Write an advertisement that encourages people to donate blood, after conducting some research.

Primary quiz 36

1. What is half of 242?

2. Is an alpaca likely to squawk?

3. Which is bigger in land size – Iran or Iraq?

4. Napoleon was defeated at the Battle of Waterloo in 1715, 1815 or 1915?

5. Change 'patience' into an adverb.

6. Would a sinner be sent to purportory, purgatory or punishatory to receive punishment for his/her sins?

7. Are you likely to be weary after an orienteering event?

8. A motorcycle is travelling at 55 kilometres per hour. How far will it travel in four hours?

9. Which huge American institution is based at Cape Canaveral in Florida?

10. Does a biennial plant complete its life cycle in six months or two years?

11. King Gustav V was a long time ruler of Sweden, Switzerland or Germany?

12. What is 33 less than 102?

13. Is 'pooped' a synonym of tired, thin or tall?

14. On 1 May, May Day is celebrated in Russia with a 'sea of red flags' to honour and celebrate the achievements of the w... people.

15. A huge Warner Brothers star in the 1920s was actually a dog named ... who had previously been found in a German trench by a US serviceman.

16. The gorilla only lives in the upland tropical forest of Rwanda, Uganda and Z...

17. A story about a plastic toy coming to life is the plot for a novel called *The Indian in the ...*

18. Complete this film title in which the central character is a car called Herbie – *The Love ...*

19. Which of these is not a 'blood' word – platelet, vein, artery or bronchi?

20. Which is the only African nation which begins with a K?

/20

★ DID YOU KNOW?

Gorillas are generally gentle creatures that live in family groups. It is believed that gorillas can recognise each other by their faces and the shapes of their bodies!

INTERNET CHALLENGES

O Write some facts about the diet and habitat of the gorilla.
O View pictures of gorillas interacting with humans.
O Name the different types of gorillas.

PRIMARY QUIZ 37 – TEACHERS NOTES

BEFORE THE QUIZ

Vocabulary
- Define the words 'vertex' and 'analogy'.
- Teachers may like to pronounce the words 'aardvark', 'salmonella', 'van Rijn', 'Boer', 'Befana' and 'Siam' for pupils.

Suggested resources
- Internet

ANSWERS

1. 12.5%
2. shire
3. 9
4. homes/lands
5. aardvark
6. bacterium
7. yes
8. 3
9. Ben Franklin
10. true
11. Rembrandt
12. South Africa
13. antonym
14. Italy
15. (in)animate
16. flooding
17. Swiss
18. army
19. (d)
20. Thailand

FURTHER EXPLORATION

Question 4	Find out which English words have a Native American origin; e.g. 'raccoon', 'wigwam' etc.
Question 5	Challenge the pupils to make lists of words that have double vowels; e.g. 'skiing', 'cheese', 'moose', 'vacuum' etc.
Question 13	Hold an antonym quiz for pupils to answer in groups.
Question 15	Prepare a still life display and ask pupils to sketch or paint what they see.
Question 18	Write your own analogies for a partner to solve.

Primary quiz 37

1. What percentage is the equivalent of $\frac{1}{8}$?

2. Which is the largest breed of horse – Arabian, shire or quarter horse?

3. What does the Latin word 'novem' mean?

4. In the 1830s, white settlers in the USA travelled west in their thousands, forcing thousands of native Americans from their …

5. Which word has three vowels – aardvark or anteater?

6. Is salmonella a fish or a bacterium which can cause disease?

7. Is weightlifting an Olympic event for women?

8. How many diagonals, leaving from one vertex only, does a hexagon have?

9. Whose dangerous kite experiment proved that lightning was a discharge of electricity?

10. The coast redwood is the world's tallest living tree. True or false?

11. Which famous Dutch painter had the surname of van Rijn?

12. In which country was the Boer War fought?

13. 'Ancient' is an *a*… of 'modern'.

14. Lady Befana is a legendary character from which country?

15. 'Still life' is the study of an arrangement of *in*… objects.

16. One of the lowest-lying countries in Asia is Bangladesh. It also suffers from terrible storms and the subsequent result is severe …

17. What nationality is Heidi – Swedish, Swiss or German?

18. Complete this analogy - Soldier is to … as sailor is to navy.

19. Where on your tongue are most of your taste buds?
    (a) the front
    (b) the back
    (c) the sides
    (d) the sides and back

20. Which country used to be known as Siam?

/20

★ **DID YOU KNOW?**

Our tongues are covered in taste buds that are separated into different areas of sweet, sour, salty and bitter. Children have about 10 000 taste buds but this number decreases as we get older, so tastes become 'weaker'.

INTERNET CHALLENGES

O Find a picture of the tongue where the taste buds have been magnified.

O Find a description of a 'taste test' experiment.

O Find out what other factors can cause our sense of taste to 'weaken'.

PRIMARY QUIZ 38 – TEACHERS NOTES

BEFORE THE QUIZ

Vocabulary
- Define the words 'abbreviated', 'equilateral triangle' and 'acronym'.
- Teachers may like to pronounce the word 'Auckland' for pupils.

Suggested resources
- Internet, atlas

ANSWERS

1. 1 billion
2. (great) ape
3. yes
4. true
5. cont.
6. 62
7. 40–30 (30–40)
8. 180
9. Isaac Newton
10. dark
11. Nelson
12. New Zealand
13. true
14. Russia
15. soprano
16. OPEC
17. John Grisham
18. (Super)impose
19. males
20. Canada/USA

FURTHER EXPLORATION

Question 1   Solve word problems using very large numbers.

Question 8   Use different types of triangles to create geometric designs.

Question 12   Write a list of 10 things you would do if you visited New Zealand.

Question 15   Listen to operatic pieces of music as a stimulus during creative writing sessions.

Question 19   Find out what causes colour blindness and the problems it causes people who have it.

Primary quiz 38

1. Which is bigger – 10 million or 1 billion?

2. What type of creature is a 'bonobos'?

3. Was *Who Framed Roger Rabbit?* an animated film?

4. The first Grand National was run at Aintree, England in 1839? True or false?

5. Write the abbreviated form of the word 'continued'.

6. How many days in July and August combined?

7. In tennis, what must have been the score before the first 'deuce' of a game?

8. What is the sum of the degrees in an equilateral triangle?

9. Who is known for the famous incident in which an apple fell on his head?

10. Is loam usually light or dark in colour?

11. The ship *Victory* was the most famous to be sailed by Horatio …

12. Where would I be if I visited cities such as Wellington and Auckland?

13. If you 'have a screw loose' it means you are crazy. True or false?

14. In some parts of *R*… you can tell if a woman is married or not by the colour of the headdress she wears – red if she is married and white if she is not.

15. A … is the highest female singing voice.

16. The Organization of Petroleum Exporting Countries is abbreviated to what acronym?

17. Who wrote *The Pelican Brief*, *The Client*, *The Firm* and *The Runaway Jury*?

18. To place something exactly on top of something else is to *super*…

19. Does colour blindness affect males or females more?

20. The Great Lakes form part of the border between which two countries?

/20

⭐ **DID YOU KNOW?**

The names of the months of the year have all come from Latin, the language of the ancient Romans. For example, July was named after the Roman emperor Julius Caesar and August was named after his nephew, Augustus, also an emperor of Rome.

INTERNET CHALLENGES

O Find out the origins of the other months of the year.
O Find out how the original Roman calendar differed from the one we use today.
O Where did the word 'month' come from?

PRIMARY QUIZ 39 – TEACHERS NOTES

BEFORE THE QUIZ

Vocabulary

* Ensure pupils understand what a 'cubed' number is.

Suggested resources

* Internet, atlas, horoscopes from magazine or newspaper

ANSWERS

1. 1000
2. swarm/hive
3. Capricorn
4. *Carol*
5. They're
6. Madonna
7. 15
8. 17:45
9. carbon dating
10. humans/animals
11. Paul
12. Indian
13. danger
14. Scottish (male)
15. opposite
16. true
17. *Chair*
18. Swastika
19. high
20. true

FURTHER EXPLORATION

Question 2   Write a playscript about a bee's life in a hive.

Question 3   Create 12 new signs of the zodiac and describe the characteristics of people of each sign.

Question 9   Find out the tasks an archaeologist performs in his/her daily work.

Question 10   Use the *Guinness Book of World Records* to find out facts about human transplants.

Question 14   View pictures of different national costumes and learn the terms used to describe different pieces of clothing.

Primary quiz 39

1. What is 10 cubed?

2. What is a collective group of bees called?

3. Which sign of the zodiac is symbolised by the goat?

4. In 1843, Charles Dickens wrote his story *A Christmas ...*?

5. Which word is wrong in this sentence? *'They're new house will be completed next week.'*

6. What is a picture or a statue representing the Virgin Mary called?

7. How many colour balls are there in a standard game of pool?

8. Change this time to 24-hour time – 5.45 pm.

9. What is the method called which dates organic material such as bones and wood?

10. Grafting is to plants as transplants is to ...

11. Who wrote two famous letters to the Corinthians?

12. What is the ocean which lies between Africa and Australia?

13. In the word 'endangered', what is the root word?

14. Which national costume includes a 'sporran'?

15. 'Irony' is saying one thing but meaning the ...

16. The Aral Sea is a human-caused disaster – it has shrunk by a third. True or false?

17. Complete this book title – *A Wishing ... Again*.

18. What ancient symbol was adapted by the Nazis as their symbol?

19. When vocal cords are close together, ... – pitched sounds are made.

20. There are 13 countries in South America – Brazil borders 10 of them. True or false?

/20

★ **DID YOU KNOW?**

Your vocal cords are made from muscle and ligament and stretch horizontally across the larynx (voice box). A newborn baby's vocal cords are about six millimetres long. These grow to be 20 millimetres long in an adult woman and 30 millimetres long in an adult man.

INTERNET CHALLENGES

O View pictures of the vocal cords.

O Find out how the vocal cords produce high or low sounds.

O Find out why a boy's voice 'breaks' when he reaches puberty.

PRIMARY QUIZ 40 – TEACHERS NOTES

BEFORE THE QUIZ

Vocabulary

*   Define the words 'pivoted', 'acronym' and 'compound word'.
*   Teachers may like to pronounce the words 'Malawi', 'Beethoven', 'brie' and 'Carnegie' for pupils.

Suggested resources

*   Internet, atlas, chart of the human skeleton

ANSWERS

1. 0.75
2. tigress
3. Malawi
4. Booth
5. occurred
6. Bulldog
7. playing cards
8. B
9. fulcrum
10. true
11. Chuck
12. Infant
13. outer
14. France
15. Marilyn Monroe
16. Sentosa
17. *Friends*
18. eagle
19. leg
20. Tasmania

FURTHER EXPLORATION

Question 2   Compile a fact file on the tiger.
Question 4   Find out what the Salvation Army or similar charity groups do.
Question 7   Play a range of card games that involve tactics or adding.
Question 13 Create fun 'new' compound words that pupils think should be part of everyday language.
Question 14 List foods and the country from which they originate.

Primary quiz 40

1. What is 50% add 25%, written as a decimal?

2. What is a female tiger called?

3. Your life expectancy is likely to be the lowest if you live in which country – Finland, Malawi or Hungary?

4. The Salvation Army was founded in 1865 by William Booth, Button or Bread?

5. Which is the correct spelling? ocurred, occurred, occured

6. In some schools the game is called Red Rover – in others it is called British ...

7. Are question cards, playing cards or dice used in the game of cribbage?

8. Which part of this coordinate would you plot on the horizontal axis: (B,3)?

9. What, starting with 'f', is the point on which a lever pivots?

10. 'Organic gardening' refers to the non-use of chemical sprays and manufactured fertilisers. True or false?

11. Which Berry wrote *Roll Over Beethoven*?

12. In the acronym SIDS, what does the 'I' stand for?

13. Which is not a compound word – rowboat, tablespoon, outer or toenail?

14. From which country does brie cheese originate?

15. This huge star of the screen was born Norma Jean Baker but later changed her name to ...

16. Singapore is one of the most crowded countries in the world, yet it has a beautiful 'jewel in the crown' called *S*... Island.

17. Dale Carnegie wrote the bestseller *How to Win ... and Influence People*.

18. A griffin has the head of which creature?

19. Where in the body will you find the fibula?

20. Which state of Australia is not part of the mainland – Victoria, Queensland or Tasmania?

/20

★ **DID YOU KNOW?**

One of the best known cheeses is Swiss cheese. The holes in this cheese are caused by the bubbles formed when gas expands during the time the cheese 'ripens'.

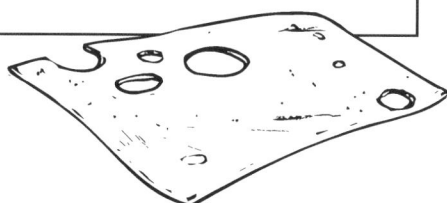

INTERNET CHALLENGES

O Visit a website intended for cheese lovers.

O Write the names of some of the world's most popular cheeses.

O Describe a cheese you think you would refuse to eat.

Answers

Quiz 1
1. 69
2. arachnid
3. alphabet
4. Boston
5. (c)
6. Blue
7. football
8. 12
9. heavier-than-air aircraft
10. yes
11. (a)
12. false
13. 3
14. Jewish
15. tempo
16. yes
17. Peter Benchley
18. incubator
19. ear
20 Austria

Quiz 2
1. 84
2. mosquito
3. tree
4. 20th
5. yes
6. aorta
7. Tour de France
8. 36
9. sound/sight
10. Christmas
11. Russia
12. true
13. weighed
14. South America
15. red/yellow/blue
16. Yellow
17. lean
18. Submarine
19. orchid
20. Sea

Quiz 3
1. 3
2. yes
3. police officer
4. Mandela
5. exercise
6. no
7. game fishing
8. 72 sq m
9. true
10. Australia
11. Ripper
12. Roll
13. school
14. (a)
15. music
16. fog
17. Grimm
18. tricycle
19. 40
20. false

Quiz 4
1. 121
2. ostrich
3. General Custer
4. false
5. spare
6. singer
7. Jonny Wilkinson
8. 1.8 L
9. television
10. mushroom/fungus
11. George Washington
12. 53
13. d
14. New Zealand
15. (b)
16. (a)
17. 7
18. nerves
19. shoulder
20. Scandinavia

Quiz 5
1. $^1/_3$
2. troops
3. Arthur
4. Indonesia
5. y
6. Spain
7. chalk
8. none
9. gigabyte
10. true
11. Napoleon
12. whip
13. (b)
14. true
15. Bilbo Baggins
16. World Health Organization
17. Horse
18. no
19. true
20. Argentina

Quiz 6
1. no
2. giraffe
3. doctor
4. Indonesia
5. off
6. 144
7. high jump
8. yes
9. hot air balloon
10. grass/weed/lawn
11. Dickens
12. Australia
13. (c)
14. Russia
15. false
16. better
17. the tarts
18. country
19. brain
20. Japan

Quiz 7
1. 6.84
2. nocturnal
3. yes
4. Gettysburg
5. king
6. no
7. 45
8. 10 000
9. Karl Benz
10. cedar
11. Hans Christian Andersen
12. (race)horse
13. gather (hard 'g')
14. (c)
15. Chaplin
16. acidic
17. *Little Women*
18. long
19. eyes
20. false

Quiz 8
1. 43
2. true
3. 1 mile
4. Stonehenge
5. were
6. throw
7. tennis
8. yes
9. General Electric Company
10. yes
11. Van Gogh
12. 50s
13. churches
14. Japan
15. painting
16. positive
17. bread
18. piccolo
19. sugar
20. true

Answers

Quiz 9
1. 4
2. greyhound
3. Snoopy
4. (a)
5. Kate
6. 11
7. France
8. 0105 hrs
9. no
10. chlorophyll
11. Sherlock Holmes
12. Edmund Hillary
13. beneath
14. people of the USSR
15. true
16. false
17. Mary Poppins
18. 420
19. blood
20. Tanzania

Quiz 10
1. 3600
2. lodge
3. eggs
4. 1969
5. happiness
6. African
7. wrestling
8. yes
9. ballpoint pen
10. (c)
11. Pasteur
12. scent
13. hottest
14. (a)
15. musical instrument
16. pressure
17. plum
18. plant
19. (b)
20. saffron (orange)

Quiz 11
1. 35
2. odour
3. Incorporated
4. China
5. 5
6. glacier
7. 20
8. 21 hours
9. Memory
10. bouquets
11. Nobel Prize/dynamite
12. knead
13. foot
14. Mexico
15. Star Trek
16. (c)
17. *Baggy*
18. 60s
19. skin
20. Mediterranean

Quiz 12
1. 27
2. bamboo
3. Athens
4. true
5. question mark
6. planets
7. yachting
8. 32 m
9. IBM-compatible
10. stamen
11. Elizabeth II
12. lion
13. (b)
14. (b)
15. false
16. true
17. Secret Garden
18. lilac
19. heights
20. true

Quiz 13
1. yes
2. ostrich
3. Spain
4. tube
5. pronoun
6. green
7. volleyball
8. 6 L
9. telephone
10. pumpkin
11. Nightingale
12. Peru
13. alphabetical
14. false
15. film/theatre
16. ozone layer
17. and all things nice
18. the clock
19. blood vessels
20. Caspian

Quiz 14
1. 1000
2. land/water
3. *Titanic*
4. 16th
5. tomatoes
6. stamps
7. Formula 1/car racing
8. 3400
9. 8 (1961–1969)
10. true
11. Mark Spitz
12. eat/gulp/etc.
13. paw
14. Italy
15. *The Lion King*
16. balance
17. bear
18. nanny
19. femur
20. false

Quiz 15
1. 9
2. true
3. cheese
4. 1523
5. govt
6. Germany
7. horseracing
8. 4 cm
9. George Eastman
10. yes
11. Mark Twain
12. end
13. around
14. Ghost
15. tuba (a)
16. temperature
17. carving knife
18. phony
19. chest
20. Poland

Quiz 16
1. 25%
2. fat
3. steel
4. dodo
5. no
6. 40s
7. boxer
8. 2.5 degrees
9. 1922
10. flora
11. Chinese
12. 1 December
13. false
14. Japan
15. singer
16. no
17. Stevenson
18. state (of USA)
19. nerve
20. Denmark

Answers

Quiz 17
1. 12
2. falcon
3. komodo
4. 7
5. discipline
6. true
7. Japan
8. 4
9. morse code
10. Japan
11. Scotland
12. XX
13. knives
14. Australians
15. true
16. moisture
17. puppy dog tails
18. wear
19. O
20. false

Quiz 18
1. 60
2. gorilla
3. no
4. 1768
5. believe
6. New Year's Eve
7. false
8. 300
9. DOS
10. false
11. Teresa
12. 16
13. quarter
14. Germany
15. Clark Gable
16. eco
17. false
18. Gagarin
19. knee
20. Japan

Quiz 19
1. 20
2. dolphins/bats
3. clouds
4. false
5. forty
6. 240
7. curling
8. yes
9. razor blades (disposable)
10. roots
11. Viking
12. Stone Age
13. smaller
14. Japan
15. Beethoven
16. lead
17. Jules Verne
18. paper
19. maximus
20. Sahara

Quiz 20
1. 23
2. sloth
3. $\frac{1}{2}$ of 130
4. 1846
5. stationary
6. carbon
7. eagle
8. 8
9. yes
10. red/orange
11. JFK
12. Monkey
13. dice
14. Spanish
15. Garland
16. oil
17. curds and whey
18. drake
19. soles/palms
20. Venice

Quiz 21
1. 3
2. ostrich
3. Thursday
4. graph
5. capital letter
6. John Lennon
7. sting like a bee
8. 3
9. heart
10. yes
11. Ronald Reagan
12. 13
13. stain
14. (c)
15. Pop
16. Group of 7
17. Enid Blyton
18. recession
19. heart
20. true

Quiz 22
1. 24
2. grasshoppers
3. wave
4. false
5. sleigh
6. failure
7. no
8. 60 degrees
9. 1980s
10. mahogany
11. VIII
12. Cambodia
13. kid
14. cous
15. Tenor
16. (b)
17. upstairs/downstairs /through the town
18. both
19. yes
20. 66/67

Quiz 23
1. 13.2
2. gaggle
3. virus
4. South Pole
5. threw
6. Moscow
7. badminton
8. 270 mL
9. 1931
10. ponics
11. Peron
12. 27
13. shrieked
14. false
15. Twain
16. 1961
17. Anne Frank
18. Fleece
19. jugular
20. Antarctica

Quiz 24
1. £3.00
2. (Siberian) tiger
3. false
4. 1912
5. easily
6. dire
7. 9
8. 2.645 kg
9. false
10. *The Sound of Music*
11. Owens
12. (a)
13. review
14. wooden clogs
15. Wayne
16. people
17. fiddle
18. bug
19. incisor
20. false

Answers

Quiz 25
1. 130
2. gorilla
3. Sunday
4. prohibition
5. quickly
6. second
7. volleyball
8. 6
9. astronomy
10. red
11. Hendrix
12. *Machines*
13. hearth
14. Russian
15. wall
16. four
17. snake
18. Norway
19. liver
20. Rio Grande

Quiz 26
1. 64
2. koala
3. died
4. true
5. as/because
6. *Bang*
7. bullfighter
8. 22.30 hours
9. electromagnetic
10. cotton
11. *Millionaire*
12. Netherlands
13. best
14. Jamaica
15. 4
16. Tanzania
17. sleeping
18. 23
19. circulatory
20. Mediterranean

Quiz 27
1. 52
2. true
3. *Lights*
4. Australia
5. adverb
6. Antarctica
7. 8
8. 180
9. Einstein
10. false
11. 10
12. smell/taste
13. sword
14. Thailand
15. pleasant
16. Mauritius
17. *Wind in the Willows*
18. *Rollercoaster*
19. sternum
20. east

Quiz 28
1. 4.36
2. nose
3. wicketkeeper
4. Watergate
5. full/filled/crowded
6. Philip Pullman
7. Surfing
8. 6 sq m
9. 19th
10. (c)
11. Pelé
12. blowfish/puffer
13. fortune
14. *Greek*
15. Queen Elizabeth II
16. hippopotamus
17. a pig
18. Ness
19. socket
20. diamonds

Quiz 29
1. 23
2. spine/backbone
3. rodent
4. 1976
5. brought
6. purple
7. one day international
8. 55 L
9. umbrella
10. balsa
11. Lady Godiva
12. true
13. you'd
14. Americans
15. upside down
16. (b) 3
17. *Black Beauty*
18. side by side
19. eye
20. Japan

Quiz 30
1. 12
2. rodent
3. Pakistan
4. 1960s
5. dough
6. lanky
7. tennis
8. 15
9. counter
10. stigma
11. Waltz
12. Amsterdam
13. mare
14. Dutch
15. serenade
16. giant panda
17. *The Wind in the Willows*
18. higher/law
19. false
20. Nepal

Quiz 31
1. 37
2. no
3. autumn
4. Pope Paul II
5. straight
6. no runs scored
7. chess
8. (a)
9. air/matter
10. node
11. Tonto
12. *Stone*
13. celebrate
14. German
15. *Mr Hyde*
16. fallout
17. Whittington
18. the lot/everything
19. motor
20. false

Quiz 32
1. 0.8
2. meerkat
3. *Alive*
4. Elvis Presley
5. capital letter
6. microchip
7. bunny/lure
8. 360°
9. fly it
10. true
11. Paris
12. Anne Frank
13. noon
14. Japan
15. Mickey Mouse
16. Amnesty International /Artificial Intelligence
17. 4 and 20 blackbirds
18. eye
19. both hands equally
20. China

Answers

Quiz 33
1. 60
2. gosling
3. Yangtze
4. 1650
5. exclamation mark
6. Attorney General
7. 7
8. yes
9. control
10. salt(s)
11. Romeo
12. Africa
13. won't
14. Jewish
15. (dis)torted
16. (c)
17. *Silver*
18. London
19. identical
20. Pacific

Quiz 34
1. 25.8
2. whale shark
3. China
4. violin
5. advertisement
6. plagiarism
7. tennis
8. 360
9. cursor
10. no
11. Noah
12. Korea
13. kayak
14. Malaysia
15. true
16. white
17. cinders
18. jellyfish
19. collar bone
20. true

Quiz 35
1. 0
2. cow (young < 3)
3. Checker
4. true
5. permanent
6. *Manger*
7. butterfly
8. 760 000 km²
9. USSR/Russia
10. carbon dioxide
11. Austen
12. Salary
13. rein/reign
14. Australia
15. (cl)imax
16. Teacher check
17. purple
18. booby
19. adrenaline
20. England

Quiz 36
1. 121
2. no
3. Iran
4. 1815
5. patiently
6. purgatory
7. yes
8. 220 km
9. NASA
10. 2 years
11. Sweden
12. 69
13. tired
14. working
15. Rin Tin Tin
16. Zaire
17. *Cupboard*
18. Bug
19. bronchi
20. Kenya

Quiz 37
1. 12.5%
2. shire
3. 9
4. homes/lands
5. aardvark
6. bacterium
7. yes
8. 3
9. Ben Franklin
10. true
11. Rembrandt
12. South Africa
13. antonym
14. Italy
15. (in)animate
16. flooding
17. Swiss
18. army
19. (d)
20. Thailand

Quiz 38
1. 1 billion
2. (great) ape
3. yes
4. true
5. cont.
6. 62
7. 40–30 (30–40)
8. 180
9. Isaac Newton
10. dark
11. Nelson
12. New Zealand
13. true
14. Russia
15. soprano
16. OPEC
17. John Grisham
18. (super)impose
19. males
20. Canada/USA

Quiz 39
1. 1000
2. swarm/hive
3. Capricorn
4. *Carol*
5. They're
6. Madonna
7. 15
8. 17:45
9. carbon dating
10. humans/animals
11. Paul
12. Indian
13. danger
14. Scottish (male)
15. opposite
16. true
17. *Chair*
18. Swastika
19. high
20. true

Quiz 40
1. 0.75
2. tigress
3. Malawi
4. Booth
5. occurred
6. Bulldog
7. playing cards
8. B
9. fulcrum
10. true
11. Chuck
12. Infant
13. outer
14. France
15. Marilyn Monroe
16. Sentosa
17. *Friends*
18. eagle
19. leg
20. Tasmania